Canberra
ARCHITECTURE

First published 2003
by The Watermark Press, Sydney, Australia
Copyright © The Watermark Press 2003

 The publishers would like to acknowledge the support and encouragement of The National Capital Authority in making this publication possible.

Text copyright © Andrew Metcalf 2003 except where otherwise credited.
Photographs copyright © Simon Blackall 2003 except where otherwise credited. Introduction copyright © Roger Pegrum 2003
Every effort has been made to trace the ownership of copyright in the images included in this book. Any omission is entirely inadvertent and will be corrected in subsequent editions provided written notification is give to the publishers.
All rights reserved. Apart from any fair dealing for the purposes
of private research, criticism or reviews, as permitted under the
Copyright Act, no part of this publication may be reproduced, stored
in or introduced into a retrieval system or transmitted in any form or
by any means, electronic, mechanical, photocopying, recording
or otherwise, without the prior written permission of the publishers.

Metcalf, Andrew.
    A guide to Canberra architecture.

    Bibliography
    Includes index.
    ISBN 0 949284 63 7

    1. Architecture – Australian Capital Territory – Canberra.
    2. Buildings – Australian Capital Territory – Canberra.
    3. Historic buildings – Australian Capital Territory – Canberra.
    4. Canberra (A.C.T.) – Buildings, structures, etc. I. Title.

720.99471

Original Design by IKON Graphic Design
Cover design and amended internal design by Suzy King
Typeset in Frutiger Light and Bembo
Printed in Singapore

Canberra
ARCHITECTURE

Andrew Metcalf

The Watermark Press

Entry to the National Museum of Australia

Contents

Introduction 7

How to Use This Book 8

Central National Area 18

Canberra City [Civic] 46

West Canberra 58

Inner North 70

Inner South 88

South Canberra 112

North Canberra 126

Glossary 142

Canberra Architects 146

Tours 159
Central National Area 160
Canberra City – West Canberra .162
Acknowledgements 164
Index 165

COMMONWEALTH OF AUSTRALIA FEDERAL CAPITAL COMPETITION

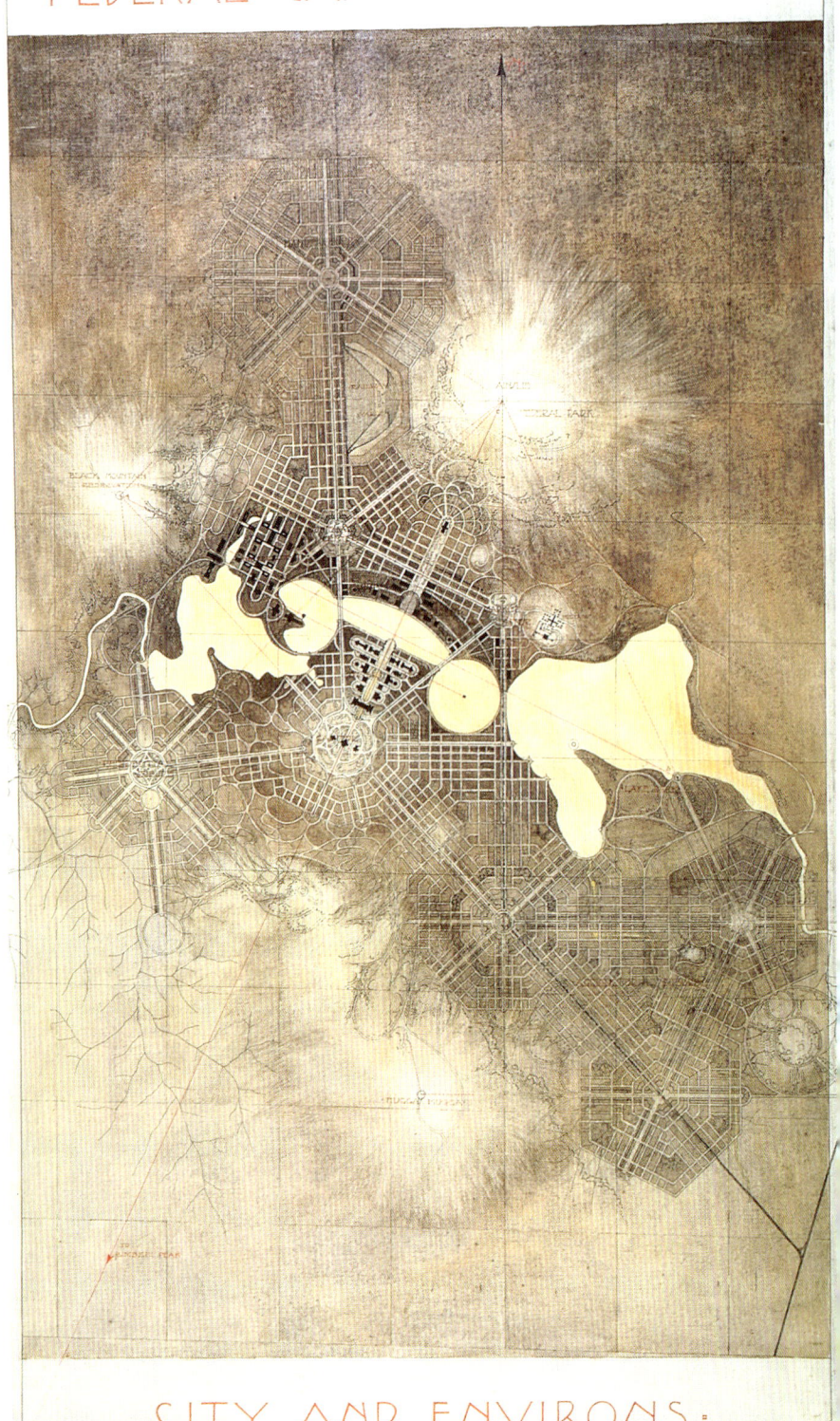

CITY AND ENVIRONS.

Introduction
the dream of a dreamer

On 1 January 1901, after a lengthy and at times a difficult courtship, the six colonies of New South Wales, Victoria, Queensland, Tasmania, South Australia and Western Australia consummated a carefully arranged federation to bring security and prosperity to present and future Australians. The founding fathers left to later a decision as to the location of a permanent meeting place for the federal Parliament of the new Commonwealth of Australia. The Constitution said only that the federal city must be at least one hundred miles from Sydney and that the Parliament would sit at Melbourne 'until it meet at the seat of government'.

There was much public bickering and grandstanding about what and where this federal territory should be. As the 'mother colony', New South Wales continued to press its claims to host the Parliament of the Commonwealth in Sydney. Meanwhile Melbourne, the capital of Victoria, younger than Sydney but with the confidence of great wealth from the gold rushes of the 1870s, said that it would not object to the seat of government being somewhere in New South Wales, provided it was not too close to Sydney. The other colonies wisely refrained from what they saw as a purely east coast squabble over a geographical nicety. If the capital was to be in the bush, it was said, it would for most of the year be 'a place of magnificent distances and deadly dullness' where 'melancholy lunatics could live and thrive'.

In May 1901, a congress of 'Engineers, Architects, Surveyors and Others Interested in the Building of the Federal Capital' discussed what they saw as some of the philosophical and practical attributes of a modern federal city. Papers were presented extolling the value of a body of ornamental water and the need for uniformity and harmony in architectural expression. More practical issues were also raised including the widths of roads, the disposal of sewage and the likely impact of the new-fangled aeroplane. It was clear that this would be a new city in every respect, marking the beginning of the twentieth century with the construction of an attractive and healthy city in the bush, free of the political or commercial domination of the older states.

A far sighted view of the future Australian national capital city was given by King O'Malley, who had been elected to the first federal parliament to represent Tasmania, the smallest state of the Commonwealth. His colourful background included a period as an insurance salesman in California, where he had proclaimed himself as a Bishop of his own Water Lily Rock Bound Church to avoid paying

King O'Malley

taxes. O'Malley became the most outspoken advocate for a federal district in the Snowy Mountains area of southern New South Wales, near the small townships of Bombala and Dalgety. In a stirring speech to the Parliament in Melbourne, O'Malley summed up his vision for a new city on the cool ranges away from the frenzy of the warmer coastal cities.

Cold climates have produced the greatest geniuses…How big is Scotland, whose sons are all over the earth? How big is the State of Maine? That State is not as big as Bombala and yet it gave birth to Longfellow. The Snowy River is fed by Heaven from the eternal snows of the mountains. In the very beginning the Garden of Eden was laid out to the eastward…This is the first opportunity we have had of establishing a great city of our own. I hope that the site selected will be Bombala and that the children of our children will see an Australian federal city that will rival London in population, Paris in beauty, Athens in culture and Chicago in enterprise.

In its search for a federal territory of its own, the young Australia would have been aware of the travails of the United States a century before, when the Congress had perambulated about New York, Philadelphia and six other cities before settling on the Potomac. The Parliament would also have been keen to avoid the situation created with the union of Upper and Lower Canada, when Quebec, Montreal and Toronto had each claimed the right to house the federal government so that Queen Victoria had to step in with the compromise site of Ottawa. Australia seemed determined to choose the site for its federal city as soon as possible and to do so without calling for outside help.

Introduction

It took only seven years for the Parliament to settle on a site for an Australian federal territory. The chosen site at Yass-Canberra was in the southern tablelands almost exactly a hundred miles from Sydney. It was not quite in the Snowy Mountains, but it offered clean air, a good water supply, a bracing climate and a fine setting for the capital city. The government said that it would build there 'a beautiful city…embracing distinctive features…worthy of the object, not only for the present but for all time'.

In a bold move, which would be repeated in years to come for many of the major symbolic buildings and gardens of Canberra, the government announced that an international competition would be held for the design of Australia's capital city. Prospective entrants were told that the city would be the 'official and social centre of Australia'. Plans and models of the site were sent to all the state capitals, to South Africa and New Zealand, and to London, Paris, Berlin, Washington, New York, Chicago and Ottawa. When the competition closed early in 1912, 137 designs had been submitted. But for the insistence of O'Malley that he would make the final decision as to the winning design, more ideas would certainly have been submitted by Australian architects. O'Malley ignored the protests of local architectural institutes that he should leave the adjudication to those qualified in design matters. 'While the aristocracy of the profession may not send designs, there are hundreds of young, progressive and up to date professional men who will compete', said O'Malley, 'they have reputations to make'.

Walter Burley Griffin was 35 years old when he was named as the winner of the competition for the design of Australia's capital city. Born and raised in a quiet suburb of Chicago, he

The decision makers on the capital competition, King O'Malley is in the foreground

9

Canberra Architecture

Perspective view of the proposed capital by Marion Mahony Griffin 1911

studied architecture at the University of Illinois and graduated in 1899. Between 1900 and 1905, Griffin worked in the office of Frank Lloyd Wright, and his early work was much influenced by the ideas of a man who would become one of America's foremost romantic architects. Also working in Wright's office at the time was Marion Mahony, renowned for her talents as an artist and architectural delineator. In June 1911, only a short while after he had started work on his designs for Canberra, Griffin married Mahony.

Griffin's work in America formed part of what was later to be called the Prairie School. His buildings were often symmetrical in plan, and his internal spaces were carefully formed on a series of levels and were austere and unadorned. Externally he favoured strong and simple shapes, usually with a horizontal emphasis. His interests extended beyond isolated buildings into broader aspects of landscape and community planning, and some of the principles included by Griffin in real estate developments in North America were not unlike those being advocated in England by Ebenezer Howard in his arguments for garden cities. In his plan for Canberra, Griffin was able to apply these skills at a very large scale.

The competitors in the Canberra competition were required to prepare one plan laid over a contour plan, but were free to submit any other drawings which would best illustrate their designs. Griffin's entry was presented in a series of fourteen exquisitely rendered panels prepared by Marion Mahony.

These wonderful drawings, the first manifestation in Australia of the possibilities of town planning, are now held by the Australian National Archives.

Introduction

In his design report, Griffin explained that his design was a logical architectural expression of the two main design determinants – the site itself, and the function of the city. The distant mountain ranges, said Griffin, were the background stage setting for the city. The lesser hills within the Canberra valley would be sites for 'buildings of dominating importance', including the Parliament House, the Capitol, a City Hall and a Citadel. By the construction of a dam on the Molonglo River west of the city, 'triple internal architectural basins' would be wrapped around the central government zone, reflecting its buildings on their surface and improving the humidity conditions in the heart of the city.

The structure of the Griffin plan was incorporated into two major lines, each of which, said Griffin, 'by a series of coincidences…is determined by the most important natural features of the site'. One, the water axis, ran south-east from Black Mountain along the line of the central lake. The other, the land axis, started at Mount Ainslie, and intersected the water axis at a right angle. Within the central areas, all buildings would be set out parallel to these axes, which Griffin said would ensure that the sun could reach all faces of the buildings at some time during the day. The government group, the reason for the existence of the city and the spiritual heart of the nation, would lie in 'an accessible but still quiet area', symmetrical about the land axis and contained in a triangle by the southern shore of the lake and two major avenues linking the city across the water.

It was essential, said Griffin, that the buildings in any of the major groups – governmental, municipal, educational or military

– be designed with proper attention to size and scale so that 'from any general viewpoint of the town [they] will work together into one simple pattern of fundamental simplicity'. He did not presume to dictate a general style of architecture, but he made clear how he felt about any dumping of neo-classical forms onto an Australian valley – 'an adaption of any historical style [would be] a caricature instead of a reminiscence of its own proper grandeur'. It would be wrong to re-create Greek temples as 'boxes with glass windows instead of masses of masonry' or to 'mutilate noble features like columns, capitals and consoles'. For the purposes of presenting his design principles, Griffin suggested a 'stepped pinnacle treatment in lieu of the inevitable dome'. Such forms, he added, had been 'the last word' in a number of civilisations throughout the ancient world. With a 'horizontal distribution…liberality in public space…and directness and speed in communication between all points', the new city, said Griffin, could avoid having its buildings 'stand on end as in congested American cities'.

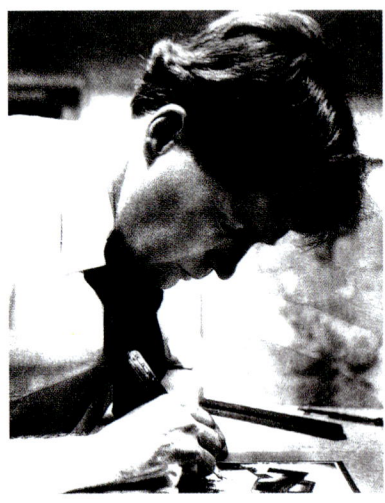

Walter Burley Griffin

It was a simple but splendid concept, all the more remarkable because of Griffin's obvious understanding of a country and river valley he had never seen. The Griffin plan for Canberra has fascinated planners for decades, and it is generally acknowledged that almost a century of advances in town planning theory has not been able to improve on its simplicity and complexity. The late Peter Harrison said that 'on paper anyone can understand it; on the ground it is hard to forget'. The greatest strength of Griffin's plan, said Harrison, was that it did not depend for its realisation on the construction of grand buildings. 'Buildings are made important', said Harrison, 'not so much by their size, height or architectural magnificence, but by their setting. It is not an architectural composition but a landscape composition'. At another level, the Griffin plan has acquired a metaphysical presence as an expression of the spiritual co-existence of man and landscape. Much of the credibility of the design, it has been said, stems from the belief that it was 'the dream of a dreamer'.

King O'Malley saw in the design the vindication of his earlier vision – 'we wanted the best the world could give us and we got it'. In 1938, two years after the death of Griffin in India, Marion Mahony described Canberra as 'the only really modern city in the world…every detail of the natural conditions was studied thoroughly to preserve them, making the most of each and every thing, so that the city could be a living and healthy and growing thing'. Edmund Bacon wrote in 1968 of Canberra's 'network of sweeping vistas, vast gulps of fresh air, superbly exciting and dynamic interactions between the peaks of hills and mountains and the movements of people…although many buildings, right in scale and location, are downright poor in architectural expression, Canberra is nevertheless a great work of architecture'. Griffin might have been pleased to hear such fulsome praise; two months after his plan was published it was suggested that he had 'been carefully reading books upon town planning without having much more than theoretical knowledge to go upon'.

The American architect, Daniel Burnham, who had laid out Chicago in the City Beautiful style after the great fire of 1871, did not live to see Griffin's design, but he too would have been pleased with its bold but subtle landscape plan which tied the city to the surrounding hills and valleys. 'Make no little plans' said Burnham when the competition for Australia's capital was announced. 'They have no magic in them to stir men's blood. Make big plans, aim high in hope and work, remembering that a noble, logical diagram once recorded will never die'.

The city was named and the foundation stone of the Capital was laid in March 1913, when the Canberra valley was little more than a pleasant outback sheep station divided by the lazy Molonglo River. Griffin was brought to Australia later that year, and was appointed as federal Director of Design and Construction. His time in Australia was not peaceful. He was peppered with obstructions by the government and the bureaucracy, and his credibility was regularly challenged by members of his own profession. His humanistic leanings, political naivety and administrative inexperience led to the termination of his contract in 1920, and the development of Canberra was for almost forty years managed by a series of government departments and committees.

With some haste, but also with careful design and sound construction, the essential buildings of a capital city grew on the plains of Canberra. These earliest buildings are the cornerstones of Canberra's twentieth century architectural heritage – the provisional Parliament House, government offices and hostels, an observatory, a military college, a forestry school, and the schools, embryo shopping centres and houses built for public servants and their families transferred from Melbourne. The architectural language of these buildings was mediterranean, with red tiled roofs, white painted stucco walls and generous use of loggias and colonnades. When the federal Parliament sat for the first time in Canberra in 1927, Canberra was described as 'a unique and interesting experiment…the modern and the picturesque blended into a composite and harmonious whole, cradled in a setting that for its purpose can have no peer'.

Progress at Canberra was slowed by a depression and a world war, but a small number of excellent buildings were built in the 1930s and 1940s. The Australian War Memorial, also the

Canberra Architecture

There are more similarities than differences in Griffin's final 1918 plan in orange laid over the 1992 gazetted plan

result of a competition, was completed in 1941 on a site reserved by Griffin for a pleasure gardens. Significant public buildings appeared in a range of modern international styles – a Patent Office, the Institute of Anatomy and a central fire station. The private sector kept pace easily with these government projects, providing the churches and other gathering places of a small Australian country town.

Griffin had seen an 'expression of national sentiment' behind all the great capital cities of the world. But by 1955 the population of Canberra was no more than 35,000, and it was clear that the place would never be more than 'a good sheep station spoiled' without government support and a sustained injection of funds and goodwill. The eminent British town planner Sir William Holford told the government that 'federal capitals are political acts of faith'. It was time, said Holford, to make Canberra a fitting capital for the island continent.

A National Capital Development Commission was established in 1958 to fill in the gaps of the Griffin plan and to plan for a rapid growth of Canberra. The Commission served the city well for most of the thirty years of its life. Its early architectural commissions were conservative, but it was later to invite the leading architects of Australia to contribute their ideas to the national capital. Some outstanding buildings resulted from this patronage, but not all of the planning decisions of the Commission were relevant to the bush capital, and the creation of satellite towns has divided Canberra into a number of decidedly unequal parts. The geographical separation of most of the population from the centre of the city is a condition with which Canberra must now come to terms.

When the municipal functions of the city were handed over to an Australian Capital Territory Legislative Assembly in 1989, the population of Canberra was almost 300,000, a far cry from the 25,000 seen as the ultimate population when designs had been invited for the federal capital seventy five years earlier. Responsibility for the physical manifestation of Australia's democratic government is now vested in a National Capital Authority. With the protection afforded by a National Capital Plan which enshrines the principal elements of the Griffin plan, the Authority has set out to foster an awareness of the National Capital in the hearts and minds of all Australians. A daunting challenge at any time and in any country, this has been aided by completion of the new Parliament House on Capital Hill and a string of important national monuments and gardens, most of which are the results of competitions won by Australian architects and landscape architects.

Canberra is to some minds the most Australian city of an immigrant nation, a cosmopolitan and egalitarian city-state reflecting the vast scale of the continent. If it is to remain worthy of the nation, Canberra should be not only a meaningful symbol for Australia but also a healthy and progressive world city. This challenge must be taken up with the same energy and confidence that created Canberra in the first place.

ROGER PEGRUM

How to use this book

The sample page below is typical of those found in the listings throughout the book. Each area of the city has its own chapter and is colour-coded for easy reference. Individual numbered entries contain standard information and symbols, as well as text outlining details about the building itself.

Chapter name relates to a specific area in Canberra

Colour-coded chapter tabs for quick and easy reference to the area

Building name which may be either present or former name, or both

Address or location including opening hours where applicable

Condition, Visibility and Accessibility of the building or site

Picture number cross-reference to the building number

Map references taken from the *UBD Canberra Street Map*

Architect or architects including any subsequent renovations

Building number The building number is used for cross-referencing within the text and the locality guides. It also appears beneath the photograph of the building

---

Central National Area

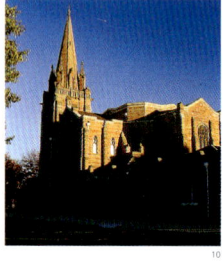

Q36

10 Presbyterian Church of St Andrew
3 State Circle, Forrest
1932 and 1979 John Barr [1932]
and John Haskell [1979]
GC, V, A

The tower and spire of this unfinished Depression era venture and its proximity to Parliament House at the head of Canberra Avenue make it a prominent urban icon in Canberra's inner south. In fact by the accident of Parliament being eventually located on Capital Hill, this site – given by the Federal Capital Commission to the Presbyterians in the 1925 allocation of 'cathedral' sites – is now closer to the heart of things than was perhaps intended.

In 1927 Sydney architect John Barr, who was then working on the spires of St Paul's in Melbourne, was commissioned and produced his early 20th century interpretation of Gothic Revival to be built in sandstone. However financial pledges made in the years leading up to the Depression could not be honoured when construction started at the end of the 1920s and the incomplete nature of the building is a consequence of the withering of construction funding that ensued. However, the well-built and finely proportioned tower and nave and the high standard timber joinery in what was completed reflect the scope of Barr's vision. The 1979 'Peace Memorial Nave' work of the ex NCDC architect John Haskell at the front of the building is compromised by a disproportionately lower budget although no doubt well intentioned.

11 Edmund Barton Offices [Trade Offices]
Kings Avenue, Macquarie and Blackall Streets, Barton
1978 Harry Seidler
GC, V, NA

Seidler's brief for this project was to accommodate the offices of separate but related Commonwealth 'trade' agencies with around 1700 staff. He responded with a five-storey building following the site perimeter, which included two open internal courts. Cylindrical access and services cores are positioned at each corner and at the mid points of the longest sides. Separate bureaucratic entities then have a 'core' address at ground floor level and are able to spread out from the core on the office floors using as much of any wing or floor as they need. With column-free, 16-metre wide office wings, this system provides a high level of flexibility. At ground floor, where enclosed space is restricted to the entry lobbies and a theatrette to impart a sense of openness and to encourage public activity, Seidler has provided some underground parking, a computer centre, hard and soft landscaping and significant sculptural works to the courts.

Although the architecture aims for an expression of simplicity and strength, a rigorous, systematic approach to the tectonic and structural systems in this project also contributes significantly to its character. This is by far Harry Seidler's largest non-tower office building and it has a monumental presence in Kings Avenue.

Buildings are **listed by area** so that Canberra's architecture is revealed in convenient groupings which can be visited by car or on foot.

The listings are divided into seven areas: Central National Area; Canberra City [Civic]; West City; Inner North; Inner South; South Canberra, North Canberra. Every building in the book is numbered, starting with 1 for Parliment House and ending with 124 for St Thomas Aquinas Church. Each section is preceded by an **introduction** providing an overview of the area relating to the architecture in the pages following.

Each entry in the listings is located by a *UBD Canberra* **map reference** and an indication of its condition, visibility from the street and accessibility is also given.

Condition/Visibility/Accessibility

GC Good Condition
AC Average Condition
BC Bad Condition
V   Visible
NV Not Visible
A   Accessible
NA Not Accessible

Where possible, an indication of **opening times** is provided, although it is important that these be confirmed before visiting. Private houses are generally never accessible but in the case of schools and other more public buildings, check by phone for open days when access is possible. Also the Canberra chapter of the RAIA [Royal Australian Institute of Architects] ph: 02 6273 2929 occasionally holds events and bus tours which visit significant buildings.

Two tours of areas of concentrated architectural interest are provided at the end of the book. Entries are **cross-referenced** to the listings.

Central National Area

Central National Area

*T*he Central National Area is the site of Canberra's national governmental, cultural and institutional function. Put another way, it is that part of Canberra which is 'of' the nation rather than 'of' the ACT, that which reflects the Commonwealth domain in contrast to the Territorial and local. Under some of the earliest legislation gazetted by the nascent Commonwealth of Australia a century ago the idea of a National Capital separate to Sydney and Melbourne and that its primary function would be to house the seat of government was agreed.

In Griffin's plan, even in its now much-changed condition, the rest of the city emanates from the Central National Area in webs of streets and infrastructure draped over an undulating landscape. Following from this the Parliamentary Zone [defined below] and the National Triangle [bounded by Constitution, Kings and Commonwealth Avenues], Lake Burley Griffin the land and water axes and the distant hills all form an interconnected system of planned and natural elements.

In this context, architecture and design in the Central National Area is highly charged, both in the expectations placed on it and the often momentous outcomes that emerge. Strictly 'national' uses abide in the Parliamentary Zone [bounded by Capital Hill, Commonwealth and Kings Avenues and the lake], the most esteemed ground. Interestingly the Griffins planned this to house a rather compact seat of government with parliament and all of the government departments together. In the event East and West Blocks, Treasury and the John Gorton Building confirm to this plan, but they house only a small proportion of the 'government departments' – Russell Hill, Belconnen, Woden and Civic have the remainder. With this dispersal came the subsequent entry of 'national institutions' to the Parliamentary Zone, especially in the NCDC period [1958–1989]. Now, with the obvious exception of the High Court, the whole northern sector of the Parliamentary Zone is dedicated to cultural uses. Extending the definition of the Central National Area to include Acton and Mt Ainslie then sees the Museum, the War Memorial, the Art Gallery, the Library and the Science Centre all forming a monumental group which, taken together, balance the iconic presence of Capital Hill and Parliament House.

The summit of Mount Ainslie is the most commonly cited reference point from which to see the whole Central National Area, but Red Hill and Mount Pleasant are also good vantage spots, particularly the latter which takes the land axis out of play and allows a nice oblique view of the lake. From these distant vantage points with their gentle cloaking of vegetation, little is needed to remind us that landscape is a fundamental ingredient of this city's designed topography. Down on the ground again a visitor to this area would do well to take in Parliament House Gardens, Old Parliament House Gardens, Commonwealth Park and Kings Park as well as the monuments.

Looking across the top of the Parliament to the 81-metre high stainless steel flag-mast

Central National Area

Parliament House

Parliament House actually takes its shape from Walter Burley Griffin's original plan for Capital Hill, which had two convex roads bisecting a hilltop circle with a pavilion building on either side and a monumental centre piece building between the curves. It was architect Romaldo Giurgola's acute insight to see that this 1911 concept for a 'Capitol' [not a Parliament House] could be adapted in response to the design brief for the permanent Parliament House and he proceeded to shape this concept into a powerful iconic form in the landscape.

Political debate about a permanent building was virtually non-existent from the time of the opening of Provisional Parliament House in 1927 until the Joint House Department began discussing it in May 1957. Within a year Parliament 'decided' on a lakeside site and this was endorsed again in 1967. However, after intense debate and numerous presentations of alternatives, both Houses passed the Parliament Act [1974] that confirmed a Capital Hill site. By the end of the 1970s an international, two-stage competition was launched and in June 1980, the winner, Mitchell Giurgola and Thorp, received the news that that they had won and that the building had to be completed by 1988.

Giurgola [b1920] trained as an architect in his native Italy before moving to the US and building a sound reputation as a practitioner and educator [in New York he held the position of Dean at the Columbia University School of Architecture] before the Australian project eventuated. At a cost of just over one billion dollars, the Parliament building, opened by Queen Elizabeth in 1988, was the largest construction project ever undertaken by the Commonwealth Government. The building doesn't sit on the hill, it is 'of' the hill and considerable parts of it are hidden from view. Its sheer size can only be comprehended in a plan view which shows the two enormous, curved walls [in place of Griffin's roads] enclosing the Senate on one side and the House of Representatives on the other. Occupying the interstice between the walls, the Executive fills in one end and the major entry and public spaces the other. It is vast: without a security pass, the public really only get to see inside about one fifth of the total building. Each of the Senate and House of Representatives components are roughly equivalent to the whole of a small high-rise office tower in floor area. As all of this space is on just a few levels, the layout of these areas occasionally tends towards the labyrinthine, especially for newcomers.

Aside from the buried sections, the tangible architectural presence of Parliament House is one of walls and surfaces where precast, glass and stone [roughly in that order] are paramount. Significantly the glass is mainly in the form of windows, not curtain wall. This all has the effect of giving the building a sort of timeless appearance rather than merely a

Q35
1 Parliament House
Parliament Drive,
Capital Hill
1988 Mitchell Giurgola
Thorp
GC, V, A

Opposite: Members Hall

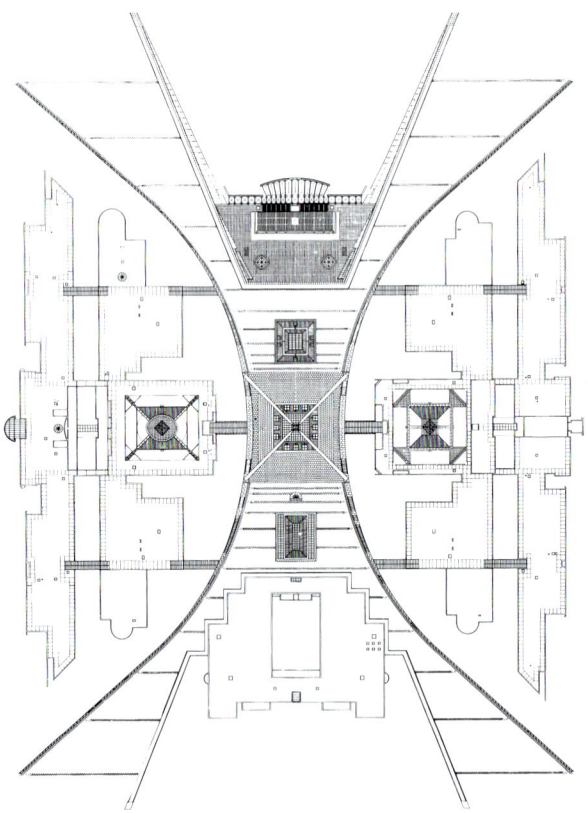

Layout of Parliament House at roof level

contemporary one. There is also a notable use of Australian idiomatic expression in parts: the front entry is like a big veranda, the two chambers have red-tile roofs, and mown grass is ubiquitous.

Internally, the chambers are suitably refined with good use of natural light and exhibit a high quality of interior design and finish. Of the public areas, the colonnaded Foyer with its rhythms of green marble and the timber-panelled Great Hall are outstanding. In addition to its national function, Parliament House has gradually adapted to a civic function as well and these two rooms particularly are used by Canberrans for events such as graduations, dinners, exhibits and lectures.

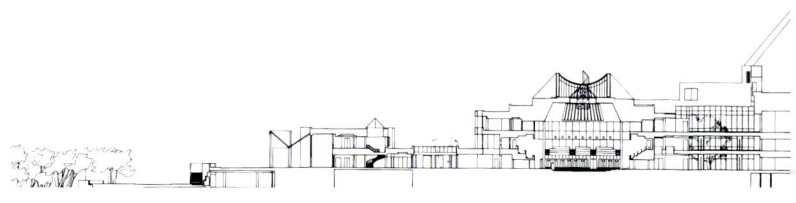

Central National Area

As well as being home to a large collection of Australian art, the interior and fittings of Parliament House are rich in their deployment of Australian design and craft in all its expressions. The opportunity to incorporate Australian visual art into the building was unique and emerged early on in the architect's thinking. Adopting a policy of using – wherever possible – Australian designers, materials, techniques and craft skills, Mitchell Giurgola Thorp either designed or commissioned most interior fittings and fixtures specifically for the project.

At an early stage the architects prepared a schedule of opportunities for works of art and craft in the building including indicative ideas about what they should be and where they could be located. In the final building, particularly along the linear pathway linking the Forecourt, Foyer, Great Hall, Members Hall and Main Committee Room a sequence of significant works is now evident. It starts with Michael Nelson Tjakamarra's forecourt mosaic recognizing continuous Aboriginal inhabitation at the centre of a ceremonial pool. Next, the entry Foyer inside the building features 20 large-scale marquetry panels depicting Australian flora designed by sculptor Tony Bishop and executed by Michael Retter in reference to the symbolic arrival of European settlers and their contact with that flora. Bishop and Retter also produced marquetry works for the Cabinet waiting room and a large 6.5m x 2m panel for the Cabinet Room ceiling. In addition, detail sections of the monumental stone staircases that rise to the left and right in the Foyer are also carved by sculptor Anne Ferguson in Carrara marble.

Moving through the Foyer and entering the Great Hall, the visitor comes into a world of wood surfaces in contrast to the stone of the Foyer. The principal work of art here is Arthur Boyd's 20 metre long 'Light on the Hill' tapestry woven in Victoria. The Great Hall also features an embroidery based on a landscape design by Kay Laurence and executed by the Embroiderer's Guild of Australia.

The Members Hall at the very heart of the building is a large sky-lighted room. Its south wall carries an important ceramic work by Michael Ramsden and Graham Oldroyd thematically based on the idea of a river wending its way through Australian landscape, life and culture. Next, outside

Senate porte cochère

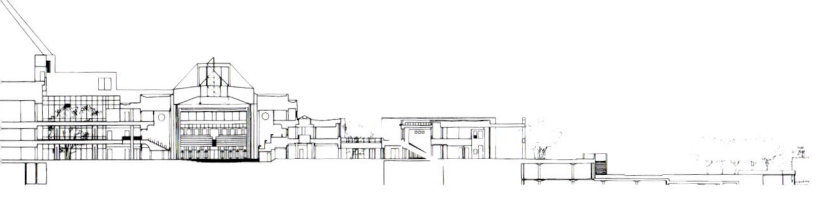

Canberra Architecture

The Foyer

the Main Committee Room, the visitor comes to Tom Roberts' large painting of the inaugural Australian Parliament meeting under the dome of the Melbourne Exhibition Building. A 3m x 12m Mandy Martin landscape painting looms large inside the Main Committee Room. Martin worked with the theme of timelessness in the Australian landscape and derived the colouration of her work from the nearby Tom Roberts painting.

Parliament House also contains three different coats-of-arms which announce the authority of the Commonwealth of Australia. Sydney silversmith Robin Blau's 4m x 4.5m work over the main entrance is based on Aboriginal 'x-ray' drawings, Peter Taylor's coat-of-arms executed in wood sits in the Senate and a Gordon Andrews designed ceramic version of the national heraldic emblem sits in the House of Representatives.

Elsewhere in the building there is a Marea Gazzard bronze sculpture in the Executive courtyard, stained glass installations to the Parliamentary Wing staircases by Cheryl Phillips, Warren Langley, Mezza Rijsdijk, David Wright and Klaus Zimmer and Zimmer also is responsible for two stained glass panels in the Private Dining room. Kevin Perkins, the Tasmanian sculptor and furniture maker, designed and fabricated Huon pine wall panelling for the Prime Minister's Suite, Mitchell Giurgola Thorp

Central National Area

took responsibility for the design of the Senate Chamber benches and the desks in all the Parliamentarians' offices and Melbourne painter Leslie Dumbrell designed rugs for the Prime Minster's reception room and for the curved wall circulation area.

The Parliament Collection of artworks intended for use in selected public areas and in Parliamentarian's offices comprises some three thousand pieces acquired from 1980 to 1988 during the building's construction period. On its own it is a very significant national collection. It includes works by photographers [such as Harold Cazneaux and Max Dupain], painters [such as Albert Tucker, Fred Williams, Arthur Boyd, John Olsen, Elwyn Lynn, Sidney Nolan, Richard Dunn, John Wolseley, John Brack and Ann Thomson], sculptors [such as Robert Klippel and Anthony Pryor] and ceramicists such as Stephen Benwell. Not all of this material is available at any one time for public viewing, but from time to time the pieces are rotated through the public areas of the building.

Attempting to take on Parliament House in one short visit is hardly enough time to appreciate the building's qualities and treasures. In this aspect it is a bit like the Australian War Memorial and the National Museum, which also warrant repeat visits.

Bernard Fisher

Bernard Fisher

David Reid

Top and middle: Marquetry in the entrance foyer designed by Tony Bishop and made by Michael Retter
Bottom: Forecourt mosaic by Michael Nelson Tjakamarra

Canberra Architecture

Old Parliament House
[Provisional Parliament House] 1927

Although it was sited at the foot of Camp Hill instead of on the hill itself as Griffin preferred it, and although it was meant to be only a provisional building until the Camp Hill structure was erected, Old Parliament House was the active centre of national political life for 61 years after it was opened by the Duke of York in May 1927. It was the first purpose-built structure to house the Australian Parliament and today it has been preserved and operates loosely as a sort of museum to Australian politic life and national culture.

Designed and built in only four years by the Commonwealth Department of works under Chief Architect John Smith Murdoch, the building included both legislative houses and the executive function of government under the one roof. The key to how this is done comes from the building's plan and an idea first developed a century earlier by Barry for the British Houses of Parliament in Westminster: the Senate and the House of Representatives together with their associated administrative activities face one another across an axially positioned hall, known as King's Hall [where, in 1945, Ben Chifley's body lay in state], with the building's entrance at one end of the hall and the Parliamentary Library at the other. The axis of course is the Land Axis, the city's primary organisational axis.

The building's massing reflects the hierarchy of significance of these major spaces with the roofs of the two legislative chambers predominant at the centre of the composition and tapering off in both directions across the front façade. The courtyards created within the recesses of the 1927 'H' shaped plan were eventually closed off with major additions in 1947, 1964 and 1970 and then the front façade itself was extended at its extremities in 1972 and 1973, so that the building now contains a network of wings

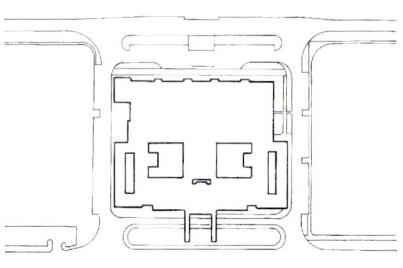

Organisational diagram of Old Parliament House showing the two chambers separated by Kings Hall

Central National Area

2

and corridors and not two, but four courtyards. In its current form, much of the built fabric and paraphernalia of six decades of parliamentary usage are intact right down to its unique furniture and fittings.

Frequently described as 'inter-war classical,' the architecture of Old Parliament House contains traces of a diverse range of influences all re-interpreted for Australia in the 1920s. For example the classical theme seems to have antecedents in the 19th century European examples rather than anything much older, and, as with some of Murdoch's other large buildings in Canberra, there is a slight US 'Prairie School' tone, but not as pronounced as it is in the hotels such as the Canberra and the Kurrajong, built at the same time. Aspects of the façade fenestration, composition and distinctive horizontal mouldings suggest both Edwin Lutyens' Viceroy's Palace in New Delhi [1922] and KF Schinkel's [1826] Kasino near Potsdam, whilst the coffered ceiling and clerestory treatment of Kings Hall bear similarity to Leo von Klenze's Sculpture Gallery at the Hermitage Museum in St. Petersburg [1851].

The landscape setting of Old Parliament House on the Griffin Land Axis with enclosed gardens for Members and Senators to either side and the nearby Rose Gardens is also largely original and reflects attitudes to the relationship between building and landscape prevailing in the 1920s.

N16
2 Old Parliament House
[Provisional Parliament House] 1927
King George Terrace, Parkes
JS Murdoch
[Public Works Branch, Department of the Interior]
GC, V, A

3 National Archives of Australia
East Block and West Block

[Secretariat 1 and 2]
Queen Victoria Terrace at Kings and
Commonwealth Avenues, Parkes
1925 and 1927 John Smith Murdoch
[Public Works Branch, Department of the
Interior]
GC, V, A

Along with Old Parliament House, these two buildings form a group comprising the original Parliament building and its administrative support in Canberra. The word 'Secretariat' denotes an original intention that, when the Parliament moved from Melbourne in 1927, each Minister would be supported by a small secretariat, allowing most of the staff to remain in Melbourne. After the Parliamentary Works Committee approved their construction in 1924 and 1925, Murdoch proceeded to integrate the Secretariat designs with that of Old Parliament House and imbue them all with an appropriate level of gravitas. Although the Parliament House is the dominant centrepiece, all three buildings share consistent architectural characteristics of symmetrical planning, early 20th century classical detailing and low horizontal massing finished in white paint over a face brick base course.

By late 1925 East Block was ready for occupation and plans were formulated to move 1000 staff from Melbourne. In early 1927 The Post Master's Department took up residency and created the original Canberra Post Office in the northern end of the building. Other East Block occupants from 1927 to 1998 were the Departments of Commerce, Trade and Customs, the Attorney-General's Office, and the Prime Minister's Department. In 1998 extensive conservation and building work were undertaken to allow the National Archives to occupy the whole of East Block.

West Block [Secretariat No 2] became available for occupation in the August following the opening of Parliament in May 1927. Over the years West Block became linked with secrecy and even clandestine activities. This began during World War II when an underground strategic communications centre – affectionately known as 'the Dugout' – was built just to the east of the main building and the association continued in later years with some diverse Department of Defence occupants. In its time West Block has also housed the Departments of Statistics, Attorney-General, Treasury, External Affairs and Territories, the Crown Solicitor and the Electoral Commission. It is also celebrated in Sara Dowse's 1983 novel *West Block*.

Central National Area

4

S34

4 National Gallery of Australia
Parkes Place, Parkes
1982 Col Madigan
[Edwards Madigan Torzillo and Briggs]
[1997 addition by Andrew Andersons]
GC, V, A

Perhaps for reasons more to do with the style of its Directors than for its architecture, the National Gallery of Australia [NGA] has been the subject of continued attention almost from the time of its opening in 1982. Something of a cornerstone in the collection of national institutions in the capital, the NGA building dates from a 1968 architectural competition for a site between Camp Hill and Capital Hill which was won by Madigan's firm. The site changed to the present lakeside one in 1969 and the same architectural team went on to win a competition for the adjoining High Court in 1973. Madigan's assertive, highly sculptural approach to architectural form making has created a distinctive precinct out of both buildings and their site setting, which was designed by landscape architect Harry Howard.

The national art collection dates from 1911, is extensive and had never before been consolidated on one site. Before another gallery was added in the 1990s the NGA had a total area of 22,270 square metres of which roughly one third was exhibition space. The building also houses considerable curatorial, research, conservation, and storage functions – all back of house – so there is a lot off limits to the public.

Constructed predominantly in bush-hammered in-situ concrete inside and out, the original building had eleven galleries of varying sizes and configurations – the largest of them had a ceiling height of over 12 metres. The effect is monumental and to some eyes, castle-like. The NGA is planned systematically on a triangular grid, which is freely expressed, especially in ceilings and soffits. Madigan acknowledged the complexities of the building, but stressed it was all based on a simple equilateral triangle when he said, 'The equilateral triangle is the nucleus of the structural code dictating the dimensions and character of the building and producing a desirable unity in all areas.'

A 1971 plan for a 'National Place' linking the NGA with the High Court and the National Library on a raised podium level five metres above natural ground level was abandoned in 1975, but by then the NGA entry design and bridge to the High Court were committed. Further, the provision of a temporary car park to the south of the building meant that most visitors now approach the building from the rear and rise up five metres to enter. In 2000 these difficulties precipitated a plan to re-design the entry, but like the original building in the late 1960s, progress has been spasmodic.

5

5 High Court of Australia
King Edward Terrace and Parkes Place, Parkes
Col Madigan and Chris Kringas [Edwards Madigan Torzillo and Briggs]
GC, V, A

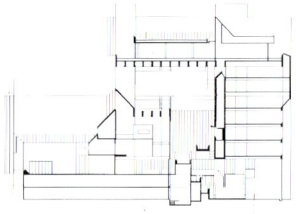

Section of High Court of Australia

The High Court building is a monumental presence; its soaring concrete columns, box forms and glazed recesses tower above the surroundings – including the not so small National Gallery – and give the building a memorable position in the array which extends from Parliament House down to the lake. And yet it is the home of just three courts and their attendant requirements.

Its grand volumetric form needs to be understood in the effusive context of early 1970s Parliamentary Zone development planning. In 1971 NCDC Chief Architect Roger Johnson unveiled a plan for a vast 400 metre square 'National Place' to literally fill in the central lakefront area of the Parliamentary Zone. It was to be a huge paved area, with underground parking, raised five metres off the ground to meet the National Library's podium level. The key national buildings would flank this plaza: the National Library to the west and the High Court and National Gallery to the east. The plaza idea was dropped in 1975 but its attendant ideas persist: the floor level of the High Court and the National Gallery were fixed at the raised level and architectural thinking about them had to match the extravagant scale of the Library and the National Place. Marooned five metres off the ground, the High Court architects developed the idea of the long ramp approach from King Edward Terrace, the large forecourt and a bridge connection to the National Gallery. This history, together with the ambitious scope for the building held by the Chief Justice, Sir Garfield Barwick, explain something of the inflated look of the High Court.

The building contains three courtrooms, Justices' chambers, library and administrative offices, a large public hall and a cafeteria space in its 11 floors. With the courtrooms and Justices' suites in the secure upper reaches of the building, the public spaces are the hall itself, which rises through eight floors and the associated cafeteria space, surely one of the nicest places to sit and gaze at the lake.

The High Court is constructed from bush-hammered white concrete, which works well to highlight the complex play of architectural forms and to give this sculptural approach appropriate contrast in the landscape designed by Harry Howard and shared with the National Gallery next door.

6 National Science and Technology Centre [Questacon]
King Edward Terrace and Parkes Place West, Parkes
1988 Lawrence Nield
GC, V, A

This slightly unspecific national building – is it a museum, is it a centre? – is a joint Australia-Japan project to observe Australia's Bi-centennial in 1988. Lawrence Nield's prescriptive design, drawn from classical precedents, began with a large rectangular prism, which has been divided into four quarters by vertical strips of glazing, then there are pieces further eroded from the quarters to fashion an entry to the east and a terrace to the north. A large cylinder surmounts the centre of the composition, passes right through the centre of the building and projects up through the roof to form a landmark object reminiscent of a dome over those Victorian Classical precedents.

Specific details such as the external tile cladding with its joints and clips expressed and the glazing with each fixing expressed, have a tectonic authenticity, which seems to be struggling to get out. The curved glass entry walls are nicely sensuous but the hyperbole of arched canopies at the entry and the tops of the external walls seem somehow decorative.

The interior spaces are effective in giving a sense of occasion to the visitor, and the system of ramps passing up through at this point give a fine sense of movement to the inside. However, the cylinder seems intrusive and could be a limiting factor in flexible use of the building. At the beginning of the century Questacon, as it has become known, still seems to be busily redefining a role for itself, particularly in comparison with similar centres elsewhere.

1988 was a year of celebration and controversy for Australia starting with the 'tall ships' sailing into Sydney Harbour to mark the 200th anniversary of European settlement. At the same time 50,000 people protested at what they called 'invasion day'. In March Parliament House was opened by Queen Elizabeth on the 12th and at around the same time the Questacon building was completed.

In August Cabinet asked the Minister for Arts and Territories to prepare a submission regarding further infrastructure works in the Parliamentary Zone [it was tabled in April 1989] and the Opposition leader, John Howard, suggested that the rates of Asian immigration be reduced. As well, the former Labor leader, Bill Hayden, was named Governor-General.

In November Canberra, A People's Capital *was published. Prepared by the ACT Division of the Australian Institute of Urban Studies, it commemorated the capital's 75th birthday. And during 1988 The Australian Capital Territory [Self Government] Act was proclaimed.*

7 National Library of Australia
King Edward Terrace and Parkes Place West, Parkes
1968 Bunning and Madden with TE O'Mahoney
GC, V, A

Although it was created in 1901 as part of the Commonwealth Parliamentary Library, the National Library of Australia as a separate statutory body only dates from 1960. The genesis of the present building is connected with Prime Minister Robert Gordon ['Bob'] Menzies [1894–1978], a champion of Canberra's development, whose period in office coincided with the 1955 Senate Inquiry into the development of the Capital, and from that, the establishment of the National Capital Development Commission in 1958. Menzies' commitment to the National Library project probably included influencing the site selection, contact with the design architect Walter Bunning and eventually led to it being one of the early major achievements of the NCDC when it was opened in 1968 by a subsequent Prime Minister, John Gorton.

Designed as a re-interpretation of the Parthenon on Athens' Acropolis, the National Library is one of the most prominent iconic monuments in the Parliamentary Zone, dominating the western lakefront especially when seen from the Commonwealth Avenue bridge. Raised above natural ground level on a major podium, it was the first of the so-called 'national institutions' or 'cultural institutions' in the zone and established a pattern of raised ground floor levels that was then taken up by the National Science and Technology Centre, the High Court and the National Gallery.

If Bunning's bush capital Parthenon has helped the building achieve iconic status for the library, its architectural manner has not been well received in other circles. 'It is an uneventful building…' declares Jennifer Taylor in her 1986 historical survey *Australian Architecture Since 1960*, '… surrounded by a restrained colonnade with some classical pretensions that evidences an unsuccessful attempt to attain the monumentality requested by the client.'

The interior spaces are of interest particularly the generously scaled entry foyer with a finely detailed stair by the architects and stained glass windows by Melbourne artist Leonard French [b1928]. The library's growing operation has evolved since it was opened with the collection becoming more focussed on Australia and Oceania. From time to time ideas to extend the building above ground have been countered by the building's unassailable object-ness so that now large sections of the collections are housed off site and couriered in on the reader's request. In the late 1990s the executive offices in the section of the entry volume were renovated by the Canberra office of Bligh Voller Nield and this presents well.

Central National Area

8 Commonwealth Place
Reconciliation Place
Parkes Place, Parkes
2002 Durbach Bloch with Sue Barnsley
[Com. P] and Simon Kringas [Rec. P]
GC, V, A

These two complementary public places on the Land Axis – Lake Junction in Parkes are atypical and are perhaps best described as hybrids of architecture and landscape architecture. Coincidentally, Walter Burley Griffin, one of the first to use the term 'landscape architect', proposed a 'watergate' – another hybrid – in this location.

In design terms Commonwealth Place manifests a skilful manipulation of the macro topography to mould a grassed 'cupped square', as the architects called it, which although not an amphitheatre, is large enough to host crowds of 5000 or so. Underneath its raised ends Commonwealth Place houses a restaurant and offices to the west and a gallery to the east, both rendered in an architecture of finely crafted detail. In the centre, back on the axis, a long ramp leads the pedestrian up to the higher ground level of Reconciliation Place and thence to the pathway system that links the National Gallery, High Court, Questacon and the National Library – an important east-west link in this part of the Parliamentary Zone

Effectively, Reconciliation Place is that pathway plus a gesture to reconciliation. Right at its centre it has a large tumulus-like mound and along the full length of the pathway there is an array of large vertical 'slithers' [again the architect's terminology] that address, with artwork, texts and sounds, specific aspects of indigenous life and culture and the ongoing process of reconciliation. The slithers are actually a work in progress and may not be complete until well into the 21st century. However the handful that are there show a modicum of architectural adroitness and whet the appetite for more.

The idea for Commonwealth Place and the East-West pathway were both recommendations of the National Capital Authority's much-vaunted Parliamentary Zone Review [2000], a document which systematically sets out options for the long-term development and improvement of the key national place at the centre of the capital.

The 'cupped square' of Commonwealth Place seen from the west at the lakeshore

9 Hyatt Hotel Canberra [Hotel Canberra]
*Commonwealth Avenue
and Coronation Drive, Yarralumla
1926 JS Murdoch
and 1987 Daryl Jackson*
GC, V, A

In response to an urgent need for accommodation, there were four original hotels completed in time for the opening of Parliament House in mid 1927 and for many years they accommodated politicians [including Prime Ministers] and staff first and foremost. This one, favoured by the conservatives and called the 'Hostel' Canberra on the Architect's drawings because there was a ban on the sale of liquor in the ACT in the early 1920s, was opened in 1926. JS Murdoch was also responsible for the Hotel Kurrajong [the Labor favourite], which opened the same year, and for the Hotel Acton, which was completed in 1927. The Hotel Ainslie, designed by Burcham Clamp and Finch, was also opened in 1927. All four hotels have been much altered, but the three Murdoch designs share a genesis in pavilion style planning and the architectural ideas of the Prairie School, whose most famous adherents were Frank Lloyd Wright and Walter Burley Griffin, and perhaps the Californian Bungalow style as well. In late 1912 Murdoch went on a US study trip following Griffin's success in the Canberra competition and, was the first to tell the American that his design was being sidelined by a Departmental 'Board'. The design of the hotels indicates that professional friendship extended to a mild form of appropriation as well.

As designed, the Hotel Canberra was a star-shaped plan of alternating one and two-storey residential pavilions radiating from a hub of the main block. In linking the pavilions together covered ways and loggias formed sunken courtyards. Planning aside, the wide, projecting roof eaves, the liberal use of masonry piers and pilasters and the muscular effect of frequent brick corners connect this architecture with its US model. With its conversion to a Hyatt Hotel in the 1980s, the hotel was doubled in size. Thankfully, much of the original feeling of the place survives although the old veranda sleeping rooms have gone. Nor can you share porridge and kippers with the state leaders rehearsing their strategy for a Premiers Conference as you could in the 1960s.

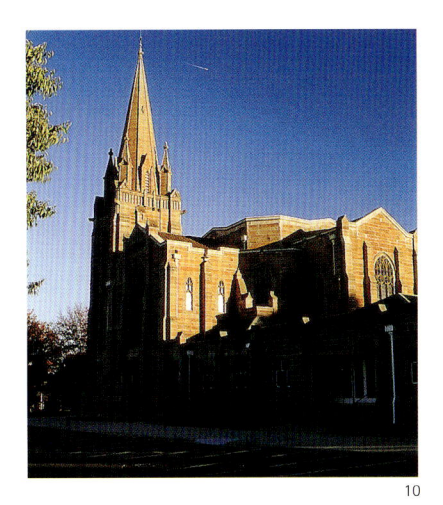

10 Presbyterian Church of St Andrew
3 State Circle, Forrest
1932 John Barr
and 1979 John Haskell
GC, V, A

The tower and spire of this unfinished Depression era venture and its proximity to Parliament House at the head of Canberra Avenue make it a prominent urban icon in Canberra's inner south. In fact, by the accident of Parliament being eventually located on Capital Hill, this site – given by the Federal Capital Commission to the Presbyterians in the 1925 allocation of 'cathedral' sites – is now closer to the heart of things than was perhaps intended.

In 1927 Sydney architect John Barr, who was then working on the spires of St Paul's in Melbourne, was commissioned and produced his early 20th century interpretation of Gothic Revival to be built in sandstone. However, financial pledges made in the years leading up to the Depression could not be honoured when construction started at the end of the 1920s and the incomplete nature of the building is a consequence of the withering of construction funding that ensued. The well-built and finely proportioned tower and nave and the high standard timber joinery in what was completed reflect the scope of Barr's vision. The 1979 'Peace Memorial Nave' work of the ex NCDC architect John Haskell at the front of the building is compromised by a disproportionately lower budget although no doubt well intentioned.

11 Edmund Barton Offices
Kings Avenue, Macquarie and Blackall Streets, Barton
1978 Harry Seidler
GC, V, NA

Seidler's brief for this project was to accommodate the offices of separate but related Commonwealth 'trade' agencies with around 1700 staff. He responded with a five-storey building following the site perimeter, which included two open internal courts. Cylindrical access and services cores are positioned at each corner and at the mid points of the longest sides. Separate bureaucratic entities then have a 'core' address at ground floor level and are able to spread out from the core on the office floors using as much of any wing or floor as they need. With column-free, 16-metre wide office wings, this system provides a high level of flexibility. At ground floor, where enclosed space is restricted to the entry lobbies and a theatrette to impart a sense of openness and to encourage public activity, Seidler has provided some underground parking, a computer centre, hard and soft landscaping and significant sculptural works to the courts.

Although the architecture aims for an expression of simplicity and strength, a rigorous, systematic approach to the tectonic and structural systems in this project also contributes significantly to its character. This is by far Harry Seidler's largest non-tower office building and it has a monumental presence in Kings Avenue.

12 Government House [Yarralumla]

Dunrossil Drive, Yarralumla
Unknown, Department of Works,
1891, 1939 and 1998 Roger Pegrum
GC, V, NA

Government House has been the Australian Vice-Regal Residence since 1927, the year Parliament moved from Melbourne to the capital. Prior to that Yarralumla Station was associated with Frederick Campbell from the well-known district pioneering family who first developed Duntroon [now the Royal Military College] in the 1840s.

Chancery building

For most of the 20th century it could be said that Government House was an architectural work in progress, starting with a substantial three storied twin gabled 1891 addition to the now demolished Yarralumla Homestead. This 1891 structure is still just visible on the north side, but is partly obscured by the 1939 stripped classical style makeover, which included the substantial south front and porte-cochere. Roger Pegrum's adroit late century Chancery addition is sensitively attached to the western end of the south front. Further to the south, back along the drive is Patrick's Garden, the only Edna Walling designed garden in Canberra. Other landscape elements at Yarralumla are the work of Richard Clough, for a long period, the chief Landscape Architect at the NCDC.

Government House is only accessible to the public once or twice a year for charitable events.

The Governor General is the Queen's representative in Australia. However in practice he (as yet no woman has held the position) has been appointed by the Prime Minister at the time.

Today the position of Governor General is largely ceremonial and the incumbent is expected to act at the behest of the Prime Minister. When in 1975 the Governor General Sir John Kerr dismissed Prime Minister Gough Whitlam there was a major constitutional crisis. In recent years there have been calls for a republic but the issue is still unresolved.

13 National Carillon
Aspen Island, Lake Burley Griffin
1970 Cameron Chisholm and Nicol
GC, V, A

Emanating from a 1967 competition between three British and three Australian architectural firms, the National Carillon was a gift from the British Government to commemorate the golden jubilee of the founding of Canberra in 1913. In sight and sound the carillon soon became a landmark in the Central National Area of the city after the Queen opened it in April 1970.

The tower is actually a bundle of three triangular concrete towers terminating at varying heights, the tallest at nearly 50 metres above ground level. The workings of the carillon are the bells themselves – positioned at a height of 30–40 metres [the optimum level for sound transmission] and below that, the clavier chamber.

To many, the sound of carillon bells is a bit dour, but go there on a misty mid-winter morning and judge for yourself.

14 Australian Centre for Christianity and Culture
Kings Avenue and Blackall Street, Barton
2002 James Grose [Bligh Voller Nield]
GC, V, A

In 1998 James Grose won a limited competition for this project, on the site originally identified in the mid 1920s for an Anglican Cathedral. With its broader scope to involve different types of religiosity and spiritualism, the ACCC has been called a 'contemporary' Cathedral in some circles and if the rather wordy name doesn't capture the fluid concept adequately, perhaps this will evolve over time. Grose's first stage building in forthright off form concrete and blockwork includes a large multi-purpose space that can be used as a chapel, but is also used for exhibitions and receptions, and opens up to the east and a large courtyard space that can accommodate larger gatherings.

From Kings Avenue the building is mostly hidden behind a grassed berm, which extends right up onto the chapel roof. Only after making the turn into Blackall Street does the approach side of the building with its robust sculptural forms, particularly a pedestrian ramp leading to the small first floor area, come fully into view.

Canberra Architecture

Australian War Memorial

P14
15 Australian War Memorial
Limestone Avenue,
Fairbairn Avenue and
Treloar Crescent,
Campbell
1941 John Crust and
Emil Sodersten,
1985 and 2001 Denton
Corker Marshall, Tonkin
Zulaikha Harford, 1998
Mitchell Giurgola Thorp.
GC, V, A

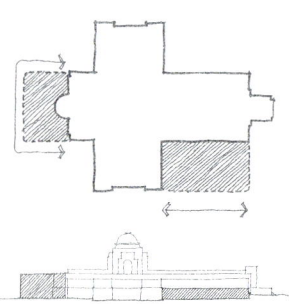

One of several proposals to add more space from the late 50s

Perhaps this building is Australia's national sacred site, or so it would seem to anyone who has been there In the dark for a frosty, candle-lit dawn service on Anzac Day. The idea emerged during the 1920s post World War I grieving period from the war historian CE Bean amongst others. By 1921 it appeared as a 'War Museum' on an official plan for Civic, whilst in the Griffins' plan for the city, the present War Memorial site was to be a casino. In 1923 Parliament announced a decision to build the War Memorial on the land axis opposite Parliament House in a spatial relationship that was compared to that of the All-India Memorial and the Viceroy's Palace in New Delhi.

In the view of judges Charles Rosenthal, Leslie Wilkinson and JS Murdoch there was no outright winner in the 1924–25 architectural competition held for the Australian War Memorial. However two different submissions – those of John Crust and Emil Sodersten – were favoured and in 1926 the two architects eventually agreed to collaborate and carry out the commission. The amended design was completed in 1926 but not approved until May 1928. Despite the proclamation of the Australian War memorial Act in 1925 the project seems to have missed the 1925–27 capital works funding that accompanied the 1927 relocation of the Federal Parliament from Melbourne to Canberra. After starting and then stopping in 1929, the Memorial project was further delayed by the Depression, and didn't start again until 1934. By the time it finally opened in 1941, Sodersten had resigned, leaving the project in Crust's hands.

Central National Area

In spite of this, most agree that the impressive design that draws on Egyptian and Classical monumental, funereal precedents is essentially the work of Emil Sodersten who is better known for the fine residential apartment and commercial towers he designed between the wars in Sydney, his home town.

This massive limestone edifice, with its silent courtyard, copper-domed Hall of Memory and ancillary tangle of 'museum' spaces quickly became an icon and the most visited Canberra site after World War II. Apart from minor additions finished in 1971, for many years the architectural conundrum of making substantial additions was not resolved and parts of the museum's growing collection were housed off site. Finally by the mid 1980s a decision was taken to move the administration function to the adjoining Administration Building designed in a Post Modern style by Denton Corker Marshall. Still more pressure has seen the original building altered and embellished, particularly in the 1990s with the Tomb of the Unknown Soldier by Tonkin Zulaikha Harford and artist Janet Laurence installed in the Hall of Memory in 1993, Mitchell Giurgola Thorp's revision of the suite of lower level galleries in 1998 and, finally, in 2001, a large pavilion was added with Denton Corker Marshall's Anzac Hall. With its fan shape set out symmetrically on the major axis and half-buried in deference to the original building, Anzac Hall has added a large volume of new exhibition space to the museum function and appropriately re-interpreted the sombre Egypto-Classicism [or Byzantiumism] of the original with a minimalist late 20th century aesthetic.

The parklands on the lower slopes of Mount Ainslie behind the memorial contain gardens and a memorial to indigenous Australian participation in war.

Top: War Memorial courtyard
Bottom: Looking south across the Pool of Reflection

Canberra Architecture

National Museum of Australia and AIATSIS

16 National Museum of Australia and AIATSIS
Acton Peninsular
2001 Ashton Raggat McDougall, Robert Peck von Hartel Trethowan
GC, V, A

P32

The approach to the entrance from the carpark

In terms of visitor numbers and the topicality of its architecture the NMA on Acton Peninsular, has been an undoubted success since it opened in 2001. At national, and even international levels, it has been one of the most talked about buildings at the end of the 20th century..

In creating the new museum the architects have posited an architecture which is rich intellectually, iconoclastic in the Canberra design context and appropriately eclectic in providing museological support for the telling of the Australian story. Although the sequence of entry and exhibition spaces approximates the linearity of an orthodox narrative, there are sufficient complexities and alternative itineraries within the museum to subliminally suggest something of the flux and complexity of Australia itself. This effect continues on the outside with landscaping treatment that includes the populist 'Garden of Australian Dreams' located in the building's major courtyard space.

Among the architectural accomplishments to be found at the NMA, perhaps the Main Hall stands out. Here, in a vast, complicated space that feels almost like a roofed in piazza, one finds a room that acts as a conduit to all the significant spaces – it is filled to the brim with a multitude of activities and functions. This great, demotic space was quickly established as something special in a city that is well endowed with national institutions.

The fantastic-but-serious presentation of, sometimes obvious, sometimes arcane architectural symbols and references in the museum's architectural form is continued in the neighbouring building for AIATSIS [Australian Institute of Aboriginal and Torres Straight Islander Studies] where a part of the building is rendered in a black-painted scaled-down version of Le Corbusier's famous Villa Savoye of 1931. The Institute houses research collections, a library, offices and administration functions.

Central National Area

The site of the National Museum of Australia on the Acton Peninsular was formerly occupied by the Royal Canberra Hospital. In 1997 the demolition of the old building was advertised as a public event and an estimated 30,000 people waited in a designated viewing area on the other side of the lake. However what was billed as entertainment soon turned into tragedy. The planned implosion turned into an explosion, hurling debris into the air as far as one kilometre away, killing one person and hospitalizing several others.

Above: The Garden of Australian Dreams
Below left: The entrance façade of the AIATSIS
Bottom: View from the east of the AIATSIS

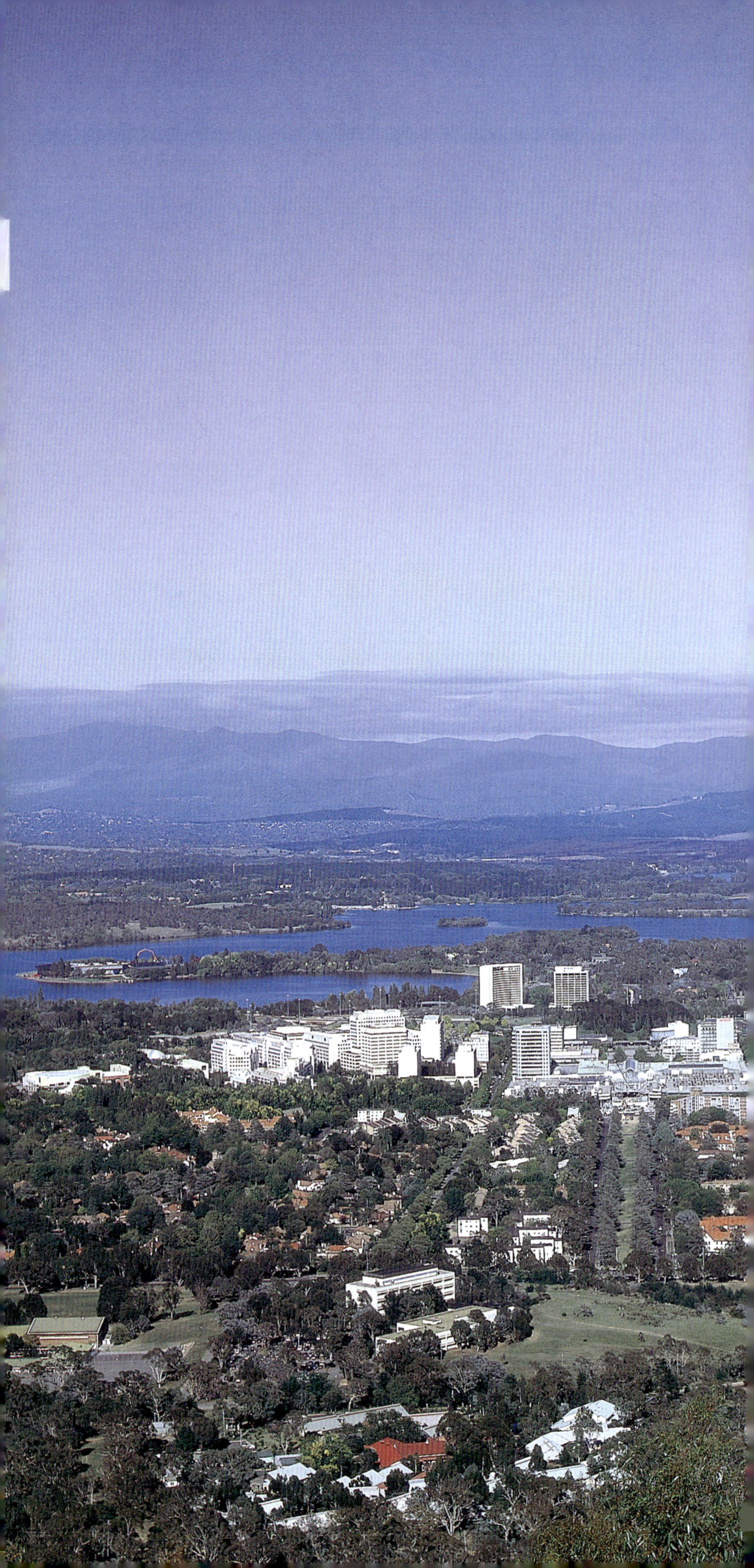

Canberra City

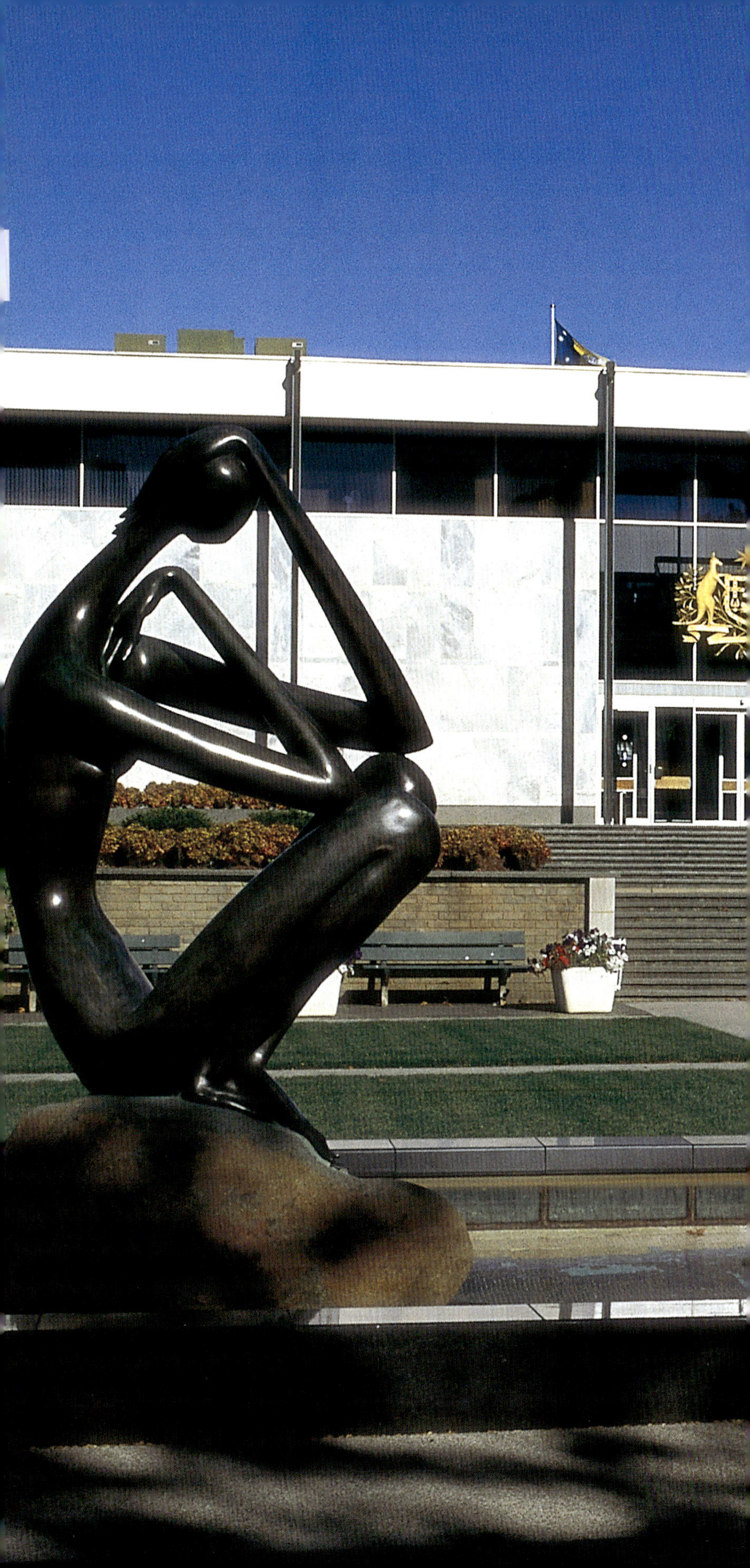

Canberra City [Civic]

*A*rguably Canberra City, generally referred to as Civic by the natives, has now reached the point of being called a 'downtown' or even a CBD. By contrast in Walter Burley Griffin's 1912 conception of a city of 25,000 people, it was to be a moderate group of civic administrative buildings perhaps of a type found in late 19th American cities of a similar size.

Beginning with not much more than a hexagonal street layout revolving around City Hill, Civic has gradually filled in over many years, particularly in the latter part of last century. Now it is a commercial, retail, cultural and administrative centre for a city of 320,000. Its current composition is a mix of burgeoning commercial entities, like the large Canberra Centre, rubbing up against a rather dour collection of public buildings dating from the National Capital Development Commission [NCDC] period.

More recently Canberra has benefited from a surge in tourism and its position as a commercial and logistic centre for the neighbouring areas of New South Wales.

Canberra City is still very much an unfinished project. Indeed, there are still large tracts of vacant government-owned land at its very centre awaiting future development. The hope is that the mix of diverse activities and the 'rubbing' will continue to be allowed so that the sort of organic urban qualities that are second nature to other cities, will continue to develop.

Dreaming by Milan Vojsk, gift of the Reserve Bank of Australia, in front of the Law Courts of the ACT

17 Civic Offices and Square
London Circuit at Civic Square
1961 Roy Simpson [Yuncken Freeman],
1996 MGT, 1998 May Flannery and
2000 Hassel
GC, V, A

In addition to its national role, it was always intended that Canberra would have its own centre of regional administration and cultural life. Walter Burley Griffin designated this site 'Civic Centre' before he parted company with the Department of Interior in 1920 and the all-important 1955 Senate Select Committee report on the development of Canberra recommended that land on City Hill be reserved for civic administration, a city hall and various cultural facilities. Designed in 1959 by Roy Simpson as a balanced entity of two L-shaped buildings and a square, the complex has evolved over time with the immediate addition of two theatre buildings and the involvement of three different architects in various refurbishment projects during the 1990s.

Roy Simpson's three-storey colonnaded buildings facing one another across the half hectare paved square are known laconically as the 'North' and 'South' buildings. Within their severe 1960s Modernist forms, clad partly in gold mosaic tiles, they house cultural and administrative functions respectively.

At the head of the square, on the axis between City Hill and Mount Ainslie, sits the 1200 seat Canberra Theatre [Simpson, 1962] and the smaller Playhouse [Hassel, 2000], the latter replacing an earlier version by Simpson.

Civic Square and the buildings around are symbolically important to life in the capital –the Raiders football team paraded triumphantly here when they won three premierships and the Olympic Torch passed through in 2000. The buildings have been in a more or less constant state of evolution since 1975 when the original L-shaped buildings were doubled in size to become courtyarded buildings. In 1996, after years of occupancy under other guises, the ACT Legislative Assembly began sitting in new South Building premises designed by MGT Architects. Later in 1998 May Flannery refurbished the North Building as the Canberra Museum and Gallery [CMAG] followed by Hassel's rebuilt Playhouse Theatre which opened in 2000.

Sculptural chair in Civic Square by Pat Harry and Philip Spelman

Canberra City [Civic]

18

R29

18 Sydney + Melbourne Buildings
London Circuit at Northbourne Avenue
1927–46 Sulman, Kirkpatrick and Limburg
and 1999 Roger Pegrum
GC, V, A

Long a marker at the centre of Civic, the Sydney and Melbourne Buildings are historically important through their being the first privately funded commercial buildings in Canberra. They belong to an urban-design tradition which favours continuous building following the street boundaries of a block, thus reinforcing the space of the street itself. This said the rather crudely chamfered corners of these buildings are much less refined.

Built in two phases from 1926–27 and 1941–46 the Sydney and Melbourne Buildings are also interesting for the financial strategy of individual developers and architects, filling in separate buildings behind the framework established by a fixed façade design. Thus each major block has an arcaded ground floor with verandas [now closed in] above and each block encloses a large courtyard space which, although planted with trees, is principally for servicing and parking. The buildings were designed by John Sulman and documented by Kirkpatrick and Limburg. Perhaps the principal architectural reference for the façade treatment is Brunelleschi's 15th century Foundling Hospital in Florence, a progenitor of not only the Italian Renaissance but also the 20th century revivalist style, which goes under the rubric 'Spanish Mission'. Further evidence of this possible interest is the use of Roman pattern roof tiles on both buildings.

They have adapted well and continued their commercial use over time, the Melbourne Building being comprehensively conserved and restored by Roger Pegrum in the late 1990s.

Griffin had planned an East-West Municipal Axis but, by siting the Sydney and Melbourne buildings (the first two blocks) at the head of Northbourne Avenue, the Federal Capital Advisory Committee (FCAC) started a growth pattern in an entirely different direction.

In 1926 the new Federal Capital Commission noted that no details of Griffin's plans for the Civic Centre were available beyond the general form on the small scale of the plan. John Sulman, who had been chairman of the earlier committee had a particular dislike of the wide verandas which are seen on most Australian commercial streets. He saw the new civic centre as being an opportunity to set an example by introducing colonnades which would, hopefully, be adopted in other parts of the country. Looking at Australia's major cities today he does not appear to have had much success.

19 Shine Dome Becker Hall, Australian Academy of Science
Gordon Street and McCoy Circuit, Acton,
1958 Grounds Romberg and Boyd
GC, V, A

Roy Grounds was a prodigous talent and this is one of his best buildings amongst the handful that are in Canberra. By 1928 he'd finished indentureship training, won a housing competition with Geoffrey Mewton and had been awarded an Institute of Architects traveling scholarship. He spent the next two and half years working as a set designer for RKO and MGM studios and thus gained an unusual experience for an Australian architect of any era.

With this dream-factory background and a well-known fascination with circular and triangular geometry, Roy Grounds became one of Australia's best architectural individualists. On the way his partnership with Mewton revived and then closed before the Second World War and he eventually teamed up with Swiss-born Frederic Romberg and Robin Boyd [of the Victorian art-establishment family] in the early 1950s.

The prestigious Academy of Science project was Ground's first large project. The brief required a large conference hall with raked seating, council room, and administrative functions. After the auditorium, the Fellow's Room was the second largest space. Grounds rather deftly moulded all of this into a simple circular plan with a ring of circulation inside and out, and covered it with a concrete, copper-clad dome. To resist the dome's lateral spread he devised a massive concrete ring beam that restrains everything together like the hoop on a wine barrel and was built in the form of a pond encircling the building.

Internationally this building is part of a 50s and 60s fashion for domes which includes projects like Saarinen's Kresge Auditorium at MIT in Massachusetts and later, Nervi's Olympic Hall for the Rome Olympics. Actually Grounds' dome was one of the early ones. Today it still functions precisely as designed with all the interior details and materials intact.

In 2000 the Australian Academy of Science campaigned for funds to renovate the Academy's Dome. Funding was received from numerous members of the Academy, a further $525,000 came from the Council of the Centenary of Federation with a major donation of one million dollars from Professor John Shine. In the 1970s Shine cloned human growth hormone with colleagues at the University of California. The donation by Shine was part of a legal settlement paid to the inventors from the biotechnology companies who produced the hormone. The Council of the Academy determined that the building be renamed the Shine Dome in honour of the donation.

20 Canberra School of Art [Canberra High School]

Ellery Crescent and Childers Street, Acton 1939 Cuthbert Whitley [Department of Interior, Works Branch], 1980 Daryl Jackson GC, V, A

When opened in November 1939 this was the main Canberra High School and the city's population was only around 12,000. Although Edwin Henderson was the Chief Architect of the Department of Interior's Works Branch, this project seems to have been authored by Whitley, his deputy, while Henderson was on a study tour in 1936. In the Griffins' 1925 Gazetted Plan the high school site is identified beside the University site, although Childers Street terminates on the northern side of University Avenue.

The original high school has a combination of classical symmetry and Art Deco styling. It has a long, low horizontal spread with a tallish clock tower on the Childers Street axis. To balance this there is a regular pattern of tall window openings to give a vertical rhythm. The building has distinctive Art Deco mouldings on the window spandrels and on the clock tower and there are also decorative friezes. In 1980 the building was converted into the Canberra School of Art and became the subject of a significant addition by Daryl Jackson. This new work has a subtle and successful set out of relatively modest pavilions, galleries, and teaching spaces, all sensitively integrated into the existing 1939 setting.

The 1980 addition at the rear of the main building

21 Canberra School of Music
Childers Street, Acton
1968 Daryl Jackson and Evan Walker
GC, V, A

The heavily sculpted forms of this building come from a phase in Daryl Jackson's work when he pursued ideas of rendering large mass in a way he called 'cubist', using common materials, particularly off-form concrete and masonry. In addition there are a number of other items which are manipulated sculpturally – things like the external expression of stairs as cylindrical tubes, a visually weighty cantilevered room at the upper levels of the building as if it were a garret, and so on. The nearest parallel to this architectural approach can be seen in the work of the US architect Paul Rudolph and his 1960s interpretations of the later work of Le Corbusier.

The School of Music is also known for the 1500 seat Llewellyn Hall, long the best used venue for classical music in Canberra. For logical acoustic reasons the concert hall is buried at the core of the building's mass to shield it, particularly, from Marcus Clarke Street to the east. The result of this design move is most obvious to the west on the Childers Street side where the foyer spaces are expressed as large glass panels in the façade. An addition to the School of Music, is the Peter Karmel Building, opened in 2001. The work of MGT Architects, this building is discreetly separate – both site planning and architectural manner – to the original building.

22 Reserve Bank
20–22 London Circuit
1965 Howlett and Bailey
GC, V, A

In 1962 Dr HC ('Nugget') Coombs, Governor of the Reserve Bank departed from the tradition of giving all commissions for Reserve Banks to the Commonwealth Works Department and endorsed a competition for his bank's Canberra premises. The winners, Perth architects Howlett and Bailey, responded to the rather constraining NCDC brief with a simple box rendered in a sort of modern classical style.

Its direct use of travertine-clad structural framing rises through two floors in the 'giant order' classical tradition. The dark glazing [the black metal mesh sun-screening came later], of the building has a severity which must have provided the image of commercial dignity considered appropriate for the day and for the bank.

The Reserve Bank building dutifully discharges its urban design function of enclosing one side of an important civic square. But perhaps its most spectacular feature is the interior of the banking chamber, which extends through the full height of the building on the London Circuit frontage. Sculptors Gerard and Margo Lewers created the large work 'Four Pieces' on the rear wall of the chamber.

The Reserve Bank of Australia has a large collection of Australian art, initiated by a former long-serving Governor, Dr HC Coombs, usually known as 'Nugget' because of his small stature. The collection began as a means of acquiring an image for the Bank's Christmas card and, although there was initially only one purchase per year, the quality of the collection is exemplary. Today the Bank owns works by many major Australian artists in different mediums including Margaret Preston, William Dobell, Grace Cossington Smith, Russell Drysdale, Sidney Nolan, Arthur Boyd, Fred Williams and Brett Whitely to mention but a few.

23 ANZ Bank
ES&A Bank
17 London Circuit
1963 Stuart McIntosh
GC, V, A

Designed by staff architect McIntosh for his then employer the English Scottish and Australian Bank, this elegant five storey stone and glass commercial building on the corner of University Avenue, is distinctive particularly because of its façade treatment. Its elevations are composed of continuous horizontal windows with a sun-shading system of horizontal projecting blades on three sides, which vary in thickness, width and spacing. These elements are cantilevered and appear to float across the façade. The whole effect is one of lightness, especially in relation to the more conservative buildings around Knowles Place across the street. For its time the building was innovative in other ways too; such as the inclusion of a heat pump as part of its mechanical system to conserve energy.

Stylistically, the striking horizontal interplay of façade elements connects this work to the architecture of Frank Lloyd Wright who arranged horizontal planes in a similar way in the pre and post World War II period, most notably in his famous 'Fallingwater' house at Bear Run in Pennsylvania [1936] and of his so-called 'Usonian' houses of the same period.

24 Law Courts of the ACT
Knowles Place
1963 Roy Simpson [Yuncken Freeman]
GC, V, A

As the termination of University Avenue and the focal point in the NCDC's implementation of Griffin's plan for a legal precinct west of City Hill, the ACT Supreme Court began life as the Law Courts of the ACT in the 1960s. It belongs to a harmonious grouping, which also includes the Reserve Bank Building and the ACT Police Building. Originally the building contained two Supreme courts and four Magistrates courts and various ancillaries were grouped around a central atrium and garden court.

To respond to the slope of City Hill and to emphasise its importance the building is raised up on a podium accessed by axial sited steps up from Knowles Place. Externally the accent is on large panels of veneered marble wall overlaid with a grid of slender classically inspired columns. A continuous glazed clerestory element and a flat roof, complete the composition, placing the building in the same architectural genre as its neighbours around the square.

25 ACT Police Headquarters [Australian Federal Police Building]
16–18 London Circuit, Civic
1968 Hassel McConnel
GC, V, A

The ACT Police building constitutes the southern side of the Law Courts Precinct located on Knowles Place. With the adjoining Supreme Court and the ACT Magistrate's Court buildings it forms a symbolic 'law and order' precinct. This gradually developed when this side of Civic established itself as a centre for the legal profession after the completion of the major buildings.

All three structures around Knowles Place subscribe to a reductionist architectural aesthetic, no doubt agreed at the outset with the NCDC. In the Police building Adelaide architects Hassel McConnel have produced a dominant rectangular box-like form, using an expressed structural frame with infill of concrete masonry, glass, sun-breakers and some stone facing. The combination of over-sized dark grey masonry bricks, the concrete frame and precast concrete sun shading makes a simple vocabulary that is well voiced. Although the exterior of the building is substantially original, the interior of the building underwent extensive alterations in 1996.

Canberra City [Civic]

26 ACT Magistrates Court
Knowles Place
1997 MCC Architects
GC, V, A

Construction of an ACT Magistrates Court was an inevitable outcome of Territory population growth and the devolution of the judicial system in the wake of ACT self-government in 1989. The completion of this building added another large chess piece to the 'legal precinct' of Canberra which, in addition to the courts themselves, has an accumulation of law firms and services located in the office buildings around London Circuit and University Avenue.

MCC Architects, the team responsible for the Magistrates Court, was formed specifically to enter the design competition for the project. They won it, ushered it through the design and construction process and then went their separate ways. Between them, the key MCC players, Graeme Humphries, Rodney Moss and Colin Stewart have produced a very three-dimensional building. It responds well to an odd-shaped site and the welter of urban design controls over this area – it is the joint domain of Commonwealth and Territory government planning and design agencies.

The Magistrates Court has an unassuming, off-axis entry, which leads to administration functions on the ground floor and then all of the courts and public areas located on the first floor and finally offices for the judiciary above that again. The impressive first floor space is generous and simply designed; a large public room which is really the heart of the building.

Externally the architecture is heavily worked with a varying rhythm of glass and concrete areas and a cylindrical metal top. On the north side powerful sun-shading forms create a different aspect, and then on the south-east side another 'frontage' looks onto Vernon Circle. Although it is hard not to see such variation as inconsistent, the architectural achievement is, none-the-less, significant.

On the south-east side another 'frontage' looks onto Vernon Circle

The apocalyptic red skies in the photos of the Law Courts and ACT Magistrate's Court are the result of smoke and haze from the bushfires of 18 January, 2003.

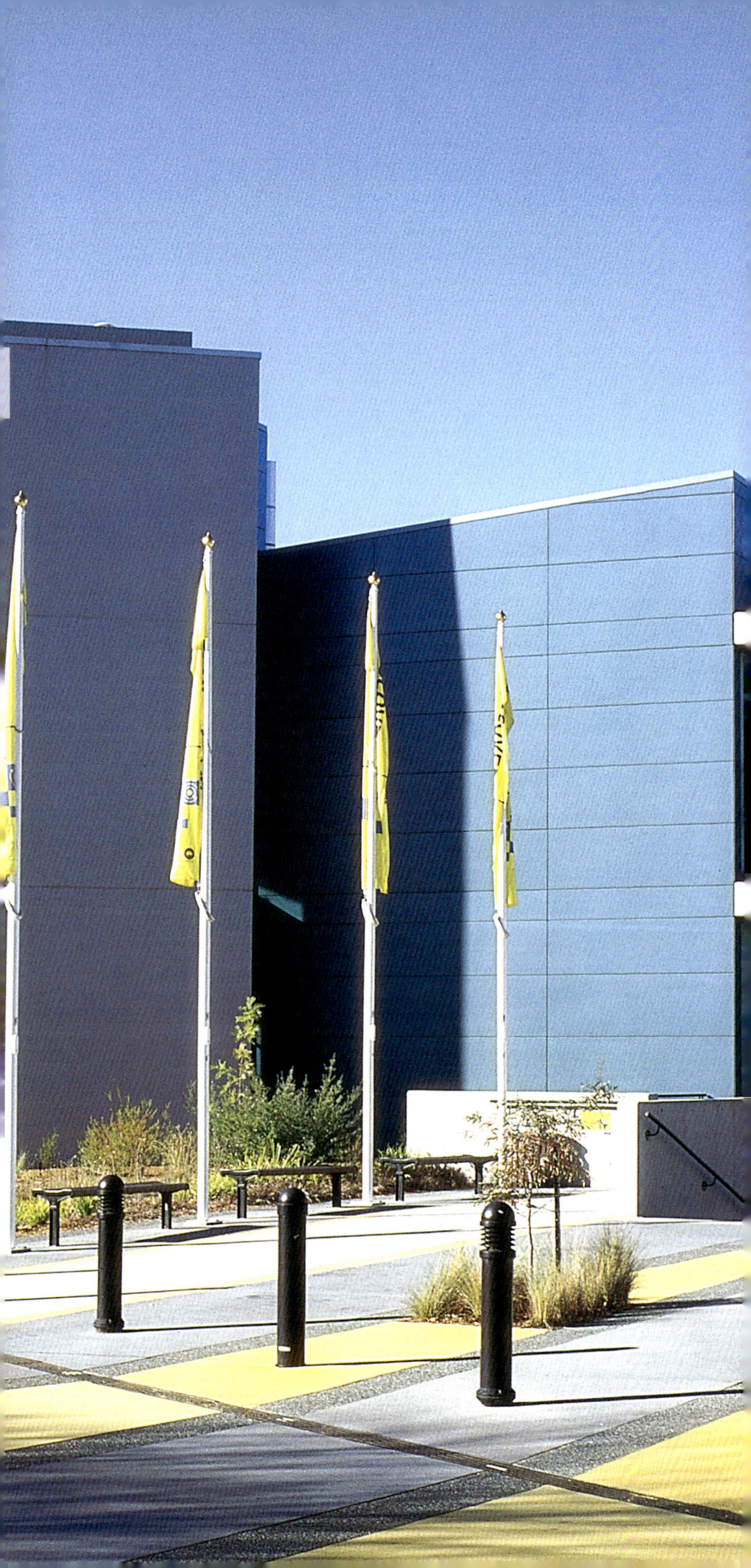

West City

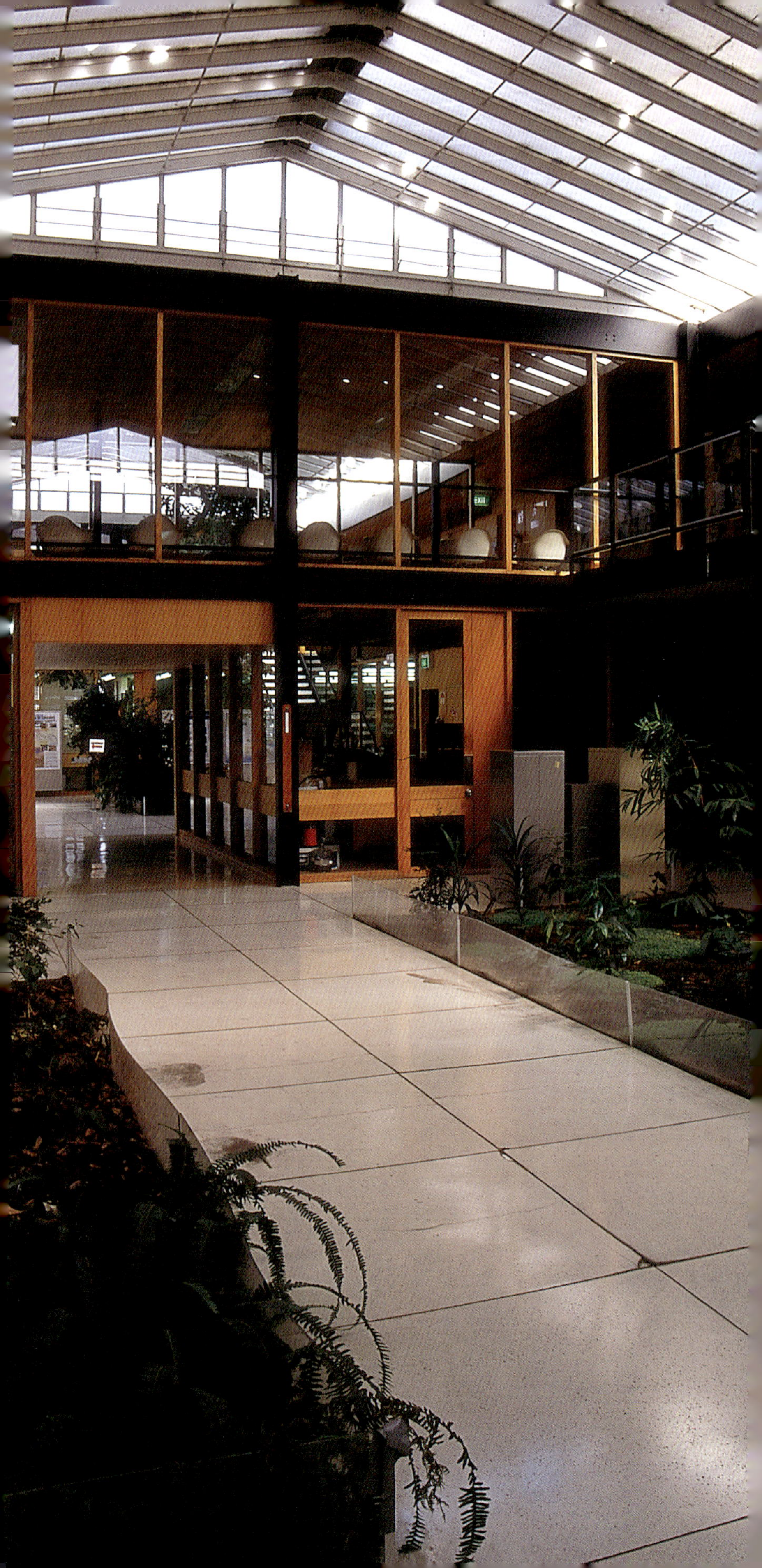

West City

*I*t is convenient to picture West City as layers, or zones radiating in a westerly direction from Civic. First there is the commercial and legal precinct around London Circuit [included in 'Canberra City' in this guide], then the Australian National University [ANU] and Commonwealth Scientific and Industrial Research Organisation [CSIRO] campuses and, finally, Black Mountain Nature Reserve including the National Botanical Gardens.

These layers sit comfortably with Walter Griffin's Canberra Concept of 1912, particularly the university, which he described in considerable detail, right down to the academic ideology. The Australian National University [established 1946] has a long history of commissioning interesting architecture, a selection of which is included here. Beyond the individual building the ANU has recently completed major urban design works which have a desirable effect of reinforcing University Avenue as a primary organising device. This is now the most pleasing way to walk through the campus and orientate yourself.

The CSIRO [initially known as CSIR] was set up as a national research organisation in Melbourne in 1926 and the following year two divisions, Economic Botany and Economic Entomology were established in Canberra. Their early years were difficult but with the advent of World War II it quickly expanded from being a small agriculturally focused research unit into an essential part of Australia's national scientific development.

In 1970 the CSIRO headquarters was moved to Canberra where it continued to expand, mainly in the area to the west of the city. By the nature of its work, the CSIRO campus has a number of interesting modern purpose-designed buildings.

The ANU's large site is only now just starting to 'fill in' and the next stage of the gaps between buildings becoming less obvious is interesting. Similarly CSIRO's Black Mountain campus is organised along Clunies Ross Street with a fairly continuous presentation of buildings to the street. However the buildings are more widely spaced behind.

27 ScreenSound Australia
[Institute of Anatomy]
*McCoy Circuit and Liversidge Street, Acton
1929 and 1999 Walter Hayward Morris
[1929] and GHD [1999]*
G, V, A

The design idea for the Institute of Anatomy presented by staff architect WH Morris to the Federal Capital Commission included a U shaped plan enclosing a quadrangular courtyard. The building was completed in 1929 and opened in 1930 at the same time as other early scientific buildings such as stage 1 of the Entomology Building on Clunies Ross Street.

Constructed with carved sandstone facing, the Institute's main wing contained administration and laboratories with two exhibition halls in the wings facing one another across the courtyard behind. Built for the fledgling scientific organisation that became the CSIRO, for several decades it functioned as a scientific research building. The original building's restrained Art Deco styling extends from exterior representations of wombats and lizards to interior fittings such as floor tiling, light fittings, door joinery and heater surrounds, all in original condition. An adjoining two-storey house, originally the Director's Residence, is still intact externally, but the interior has been converted into offices.

In October 1984 the building became home to the National Film and Sound Archive [now the National Screen and Sound Archive] and it was under this incarnation that the fourth side of the quadrangle, facing Liversidge Street, was built to the design of GHD Architects.

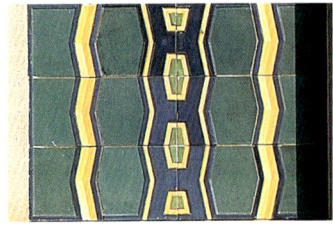

Detail from the external window surrounds

The suburb of Acton, now mainly occupied by the Australian National University, was the first area settled by Europeans on the Limestone Plains. The land was inhabited by the Ngunnawal people and the early settlers appear to have called it 'Canberry', being an approximation of the word Canberra meaning a meeting place. The name Acton was given to it by the second owner of the property, Lieutenant Arthur Jeffreys in 1843 after a town in Wales.

A number of names were proposed for the new capital including Shakespeare, Circle City and Kangaremu but there was little likelihood of any one being accepted in place of Canberra.

28 ANU University House
*Balmain Crescent and
Liversidge Street, Acton
1953 Brian Lewis*
G, V, A

Legislation to establish the Australian National University was gazetted in 1946 and by the time the first Master Plan for the Acton site appeared in 1948, University House was identified. In fact it was one of the first buildings constructed on what was then the campus of the University College of the University of Melbourne. Professor Brian Lewis prepared the Master Plan and then designed University House using the format of traditional Oxbridge college quads with an enclosed semi-private space. This is created out of a quadrangle of student residential accommodation, dining rooms, chapel, administration and fellows' rooms. Opened by the Duke of Edinburgh in 1954, University House chimes faintly with the idea of the medieval university. However Lewis sensitively updated this model to create a slightly different, more contemporary version. Logical planning locates walk-up residential accommodation around three sides of the quad and puts everything else in the fourth side which is a gentle, slightly curved, single storey building embellished with a full length pool and shading veranda on the courtyard side. Brickwork is rendered above its base, windows are metal and generally covered with wide eaves and the roof is tiled or copper clad. Floors in public areas are terrazzo or parquetry. A Tom Bass sculpture sits at one side of the main entry doors.

Here, as University House legend has it, Rhodes Scholar and future Prime Minister Bob Hawke set a long standing record for the fastest time downing a 'yard' of ale.

In architectural politics it may be that the anointing of Melbourne architect Brian Lewis' University House with the coveted Sulman Award in 1953 represented something of a conservative reaction. Certainly it was a step back from the radicalism of Harry Seidler's progressive Rose Seidler house on Sydney's North Shore which received so much attention when it won the Sulman in 1951. Some architects appear to have responded by espousing more conservative, traditional architecture. Lewis' University House and Lundquist's Royal Swedish Legation [1952 Sulman] with their simple, traditional forms, traditional materials and construction technology at the expense of then current fads and fashions exemplify that tendency.

University House is one of several ANU buildings still containing the purpose-made furniture of Melbourne designer Fred Ward. His signature style of clear-finished wooden couches, chairs, tables and fittings have been in continuous use since 1954.

29 ANU Jaeger Building 6
[Research School of Earth Sciences]
Mills Road, Acton
1959 and 1964 Collard Clarke and Jackson
G, V, NA

The original Jaeger Building at the southern end of ANU's campus is an exemplary illustration of the vertical 'layering' of architectural form, a technique that has its origins in Classicism, but here the aesthetic is decidedly mid-20th century modern. Starting from the ground, the first of three layers is the perforated brick base with extra thick walls and small openings to emphasise its great visual mass; the next layer, a continuous glass clerestory is the antithesis of the massive walls it sits on, and allows significant light to flood the interior; a roof is the third layer, it is a light and elegant folded metal structural form that hovers over the glass.

The brick base is perforated with smallish openings in an apparently random pattern. But almost certainly these are derived from the exigencies of particular internal rooms and their need for light and ventilation. Finally, on the north façade, the glass layer carries right down to the ground, splitting the brick box in half. It is all quite subtle and accomplished architecture. Interestingly Collard Clarke and Jackson don't appear to have mined this seam further in the significant body of work they have produced in Canberra since.

30 ANU Graduate Management Programs Facility
[Sir Roland Wilson Building]
McCoy Circuit, Acton
1999 Daryl Jackson, Alastair Swayn
G, V, NA

Located in a significant position adjacent to ScreenSound Australia and the Shine Dome, this three-level building houses staff and students for the Asia Management Centre and the Graduate Program in Public Policy. It has two separate wings connected by an atrium which serves as the central circulation and the social focus for the complex.

The facility adapts to its sloping site through the plan form wrapping gently around a forecourt set at a level just below the road. Its bold cantilevering and canted forms clad in factory-finished fibre-cement provide an appropriate architectural set-piece in the company of the ScreenSound and Shine buildings. This effect is augmented by the muted grey-green colouration of the external cladding, which also reflects the native landscaping of the site.

31 ANU RG Menzies Building
[University Library]
McDonald Road, Acton
1963 J Scarborough and Collard Clarke and Jackson
G, V, A

There is an obvious design rationale in dividing a large library into catalogue and reference areas, which require a high level of public access on the one hand, and book stacks on the other, which have a relatively lighter public access imperative. In a library thus arranged the visitor goes from the general to the particular, from the explanatory stage to the particularity of a specific shelved item. The RG Menzies Building, otherwise known as the University Library, exemplifies this logical strategy and, what's more, extends it into providing separate architectural icons for each of these two major parts.

The catalogue and reference area is housed in a broad, low-level structure occupying a lower ground level constructed with battered walls of concrete and stone, and a main ground floor pavilion built in a grided structure of reinforced concrete mushroom columns. By contrast the three-storey stacks element is a simple, stone-faced rectangular prism with a regular fenestration pattern of small windows.

On a dominant site, open to the south and on axis with neighbouring University House, the University Library – with its full-bodied stone base course and the interplay of the two main elements – is an important campus landmark.

32 ANU Pauline Griffin Building
[original ANU Union]
Ellery Crescent, Acton
1964 Sydney Ancher [Ancher Mortlock and Murray]
G, V, A

In a unique arrangement the ANU Union is literally a union of staff and students, not just students as is more often the case. As the initial ANU Union Building, this Late International Style, three-storey structure, is therefore important in the history of the university and its alumni. It is also significant in architectural terms because it has the signs of being designed by Sydney Ancher, an important early Modernist in the history of 20th century Australian architecture. It has [or had] elements of Ancher's architectural language that are like handwriting. These include curved walls in binary opposition to a surrounding, a context of straight ones, stairs that are sculptural forms offset against the building as background, a flat roof, a white colour scheme, and irregular fenestration patterns in predominantly solid walls.

Inevitably the building has been altered since the relocation of the ANU Union to its present site in the late 1970s. Although much of the innovative open planning has been eradicated, the terraces with their emphatic horizontal lines persist and the work still has a commendable overall architectural character.

33 ANU Toad Hall
Kingsley Street and Barry Drive, Acton
1977 John Andrews
G, V, NA

Designed by John Andrews, who was also the architect for the University of Canberra's 'Eggcrate' residences [opened in 1975, designed 1972], Toad Hall belongs to the self-catering model of student accommodation. In this, students have individual rooms but share kitchens, bathrooms and common rooms – there are no large kitchens or dining halls as there are in traditional student residences.

This project is one of the few examples of Andrews' additive style of plan making anywhere. In a concept first developed by the architect for a similar project at Guelph University in Canada, the basic building block here is a handful of rooms grouped around shared facilities like petals around the stamens and pistil of a flower. These groupings are attached to stair towers like branches to a tree trunk and then aggregated together vertically over four floors and laterally along the bank of Sullivan's Creek to make a wall of building. On any one floor it is possible to circulate horizontally by moving though the stair landings that are all connected to common rooms [the stamen and pistil], thus avoiding the banality of long residential corridors. Primary circulation and address however are really derived from the stair tower, in a manner like Louis Kahn's Bryn Mawr student residence in Pennsylvania [1965], the most obvious antecedent for the additive mode of design.

Although the forms are muscularly wrought in reinforced concrete and common bricks the exterior architecture of an additive plan building pretty much designs itself, once the basic unit is established and one begins adding them to one another.

During construction, students already on campus nicknamed the new residence Toad Hall because of its grand setting beside the creek on rolling lawns.

The name stuck and became the Hall's official title, proudly proclaimed on signage which can be seen clearly from the road when approaching the building.

> Rounding a bend in the river, they came in sight of a handsome, dignified old house of mellowed red brick, with well-kept lawns reaching down to the water's edge. 'There's Toad Hall,' said the Rat …
>
> … 'Finest house on the whole river,' cried Toad boisterously. 'Or anywhere else, for that matter,' he could not help adding.
>
> Wind in the Willows, *Kenneth Grahame*

34 CSIRO Discovery Centre
Clunies Ross Street, Black Mountain
1999 Daryl Jackson Alastair Swayn
G, V, A

CSIRO Discovery provides a dramatic central focus, and a public point of connection to the CSIRO's Black Mountain 'campus' that hadn't existed hitherto. Public areas include

34

exhibition space, a staff and public café, a retail outlet, credit union and conference facilities. In addition to this public portal role, the building houses a bio-molecular research facility spread across two levels of laboratory accommodation.

All of these facilities relate spatially to a large glass atrium designed as a key central space in the building's operation. Above and around this a welter of significant walls and roofs constructed from louvre-shaded glass, creates a sense of transparency that clearly strikes a chord with the nature of the many glass houses on the Black Mountain site. There are also views in and views out of the building which help to maintain lines of sight through the CSIRO campus to Black Mountain in one direction and back over the city in the other.

The interior public spaces of this building [below] are an important part of the experience and should not be missed.

John Gollings

The name Weston frequently appears in Canberra for gardens, freeways and parks and mostly relates to Charles Weston the Superintendent of Parks, Gardens and Afforestation from 1913 to 1926. Originally from England, Weston had been an assistant to Joseph Maiden at the Botanic Gardens in Sydney and whilst there was probably influenced by John Sulman's ideas on the need for parks and trees in urban areas. Sulman thought that an avenue or street should only be planted with one species of tree and in general Weston followed this precept. Weston's influence can be seen most clearly in the older suburbs where the main avenues are lined with majestic native trees, many residential streets have imported evergreens, and lesser streets and small parks have deciduous trees (usually plane trees).

Weston Park on the southern shore of Lake Burley Griffin is notable for its central drive which is lined by Atlas cedar and black locust trees and its European park-like atmosphere with spinneys and copses. Another interesting project of Weston's was the cork oak plantation at Green Hills on the west side of Black Mountain. Walter Burley Griffin sent him some acorns to test in the local soil and these, together with some others from a tree at Duntroon, became the nucleus of the plantation. It is now listed on the register of the National Estate.

Weston Creek however was named after a one-time superintendent of Hyde Park Barracks, Sydney.

35 CSIRO FC Pye Laboratories
Dickson Way, off Clunies Ross Street, Black Mountain
1966 Ken Woolley [Ancher Mortlock Murray and Woolley]
G, V, NA

Designed from the inside out, this building is intended for a community of researchers and administrators requiring a combination of lab-based research, office and meeting functions. Woolley has paid particular attention to providing appropriate architectural support for the idea of a working 'community.' He does this with a glazed roof atrium plan that positions most offices and labs around the perimeter in visual contact with each other. The building entry leads directly into this space and then up stairs to circulation galleries, executive offices and a conference room.

Outside, this is all neatly contained in a relatively simple concrete masonry shell with a broad, floating roof underpinned by a continuous clerestory window. There are cantilevered corners, timber lined soffits and a fully cantilevered off-form concrete stair that gives a sculptural effect to one side of the building. Nicely controlled, the Pye Laboratories have an affinity with the public library at Gordon, on Sydney's North Shore, that was built by the same architects around the same time.

36 Civic Zone Substation
Firth Road, Black Mountain
c1965 Roy Grounds [Grounds Romberg and Boyd]
G, V, NA

In the body of Roy Ground's Canberra work this prosaic little building reaches a level of architectural resolution almost bar none. Quite possibly for Grounds the utilitarian brief has permitted an uncompromising visual firmness that the residential, and even religious, buildings did not. Whatever the reason, this well-proportioned, steel-framed brick box set on the lower slopes of Black Mountain, is worth a visit.

It is rectangular in plan with one long side – the entry side – recessed and clerestoried under a flat roof and wrapped around the corners. The other main wall is flush with the eaves and fenestrated with crisp and minimal vertical slit windows. In an unusual gesture, ground level arches, in-filled with finely patterned concrete, support the building on the 'flush' side where it emerges out of the sloping site. The substation building is very rigorous and obviously thematic in the context of Ground's work, which includes the much larger gallery in Melbourne.

A12
37 CSIRO Phytotron Building
Clunies Ross Street, Black Mountain
1963 Grounds Romberg and Boyd
G, V, NA

Built as a 'controlled environmental research laboratory', this unusual building was erected for the CSIRO's Division of Plant Industry to simulate a full range of Australian climatic conditions for plant research under laboratory, as distinct from field, conditions. It was built to be fully airtight and to operate with a reverse cycle heat pump system. The ground floor contains administration offices, laboratories, work rooms and mechanical plant and the first floor mezzanine accommodates more labs, work rooms and a long range of glass houses facing north which are a dominant feature of the building's exterior form.

Apart from the elevated glass houses, the Phytotron's most noticeable architectural features are the extensive use of stack bonded concrete masonry for exterior walling and the white 'square tube' window and door surround elements. These appear to denote rooms intended for human, as distinct from plant, occupation. This excusable little exercise in visual smugness is contemporaneous with the practices of the 1960s Japanese 'Metabolist' group of architectural avant-gardists, who used similar tube forms on their building facades.

Black Mountain, on the eastern slopes of which are the CSIRO research laboratories, is also the location of the Australian National Botanic Gardens. It includes flora from all over the continent and maintains different ecosystems such as a rainforest gully made possible by 2000 fine mist sprays. A bust of the botanist, Sir Joseph Banks who travelled with Captain Cook on his 1768 voyage is located on the path to the Information Centre. Banks was one of the first Europeans to witness tattooing in the Pacific islands and returned to England sporting a small butterfly tattoo on his left buttock.

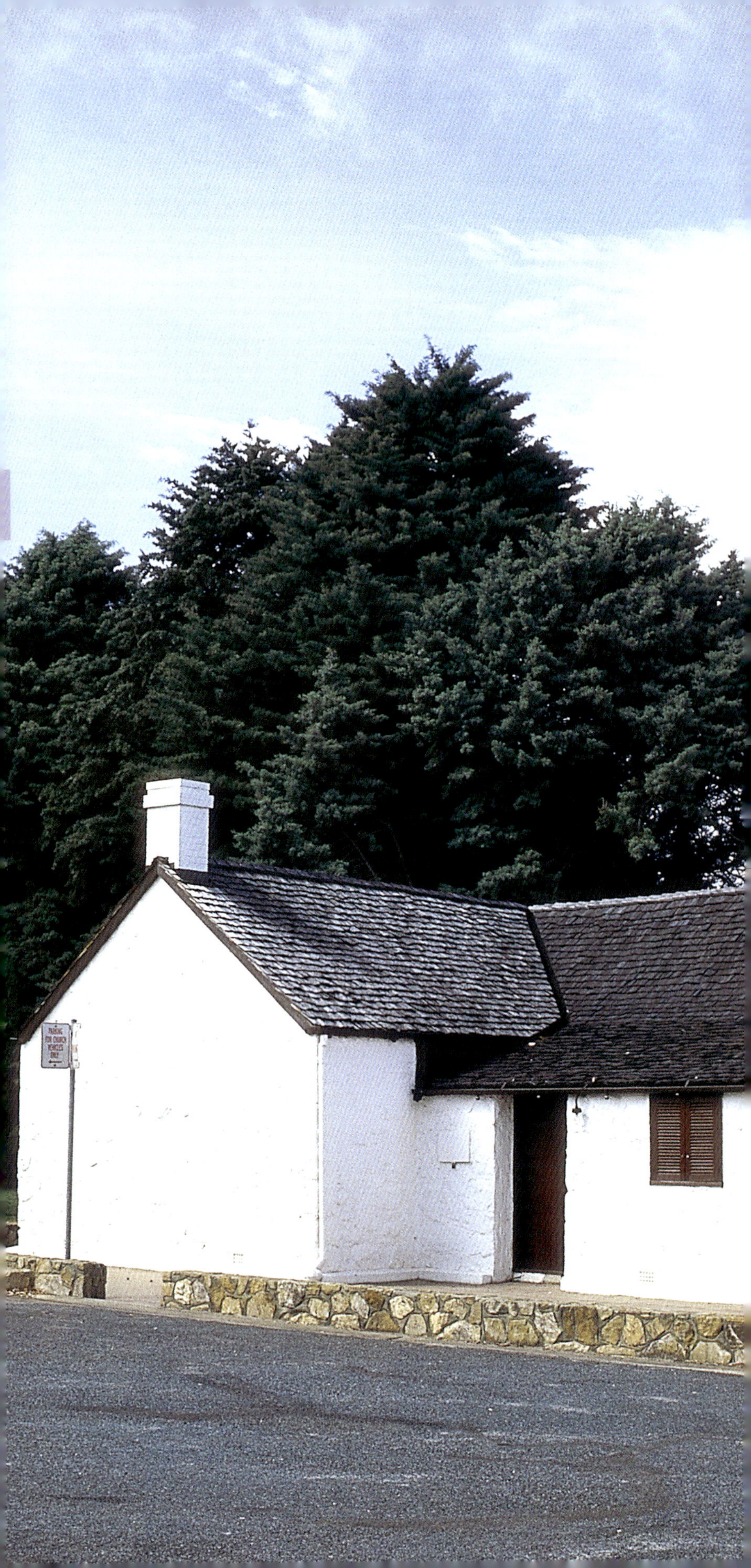

Inner North

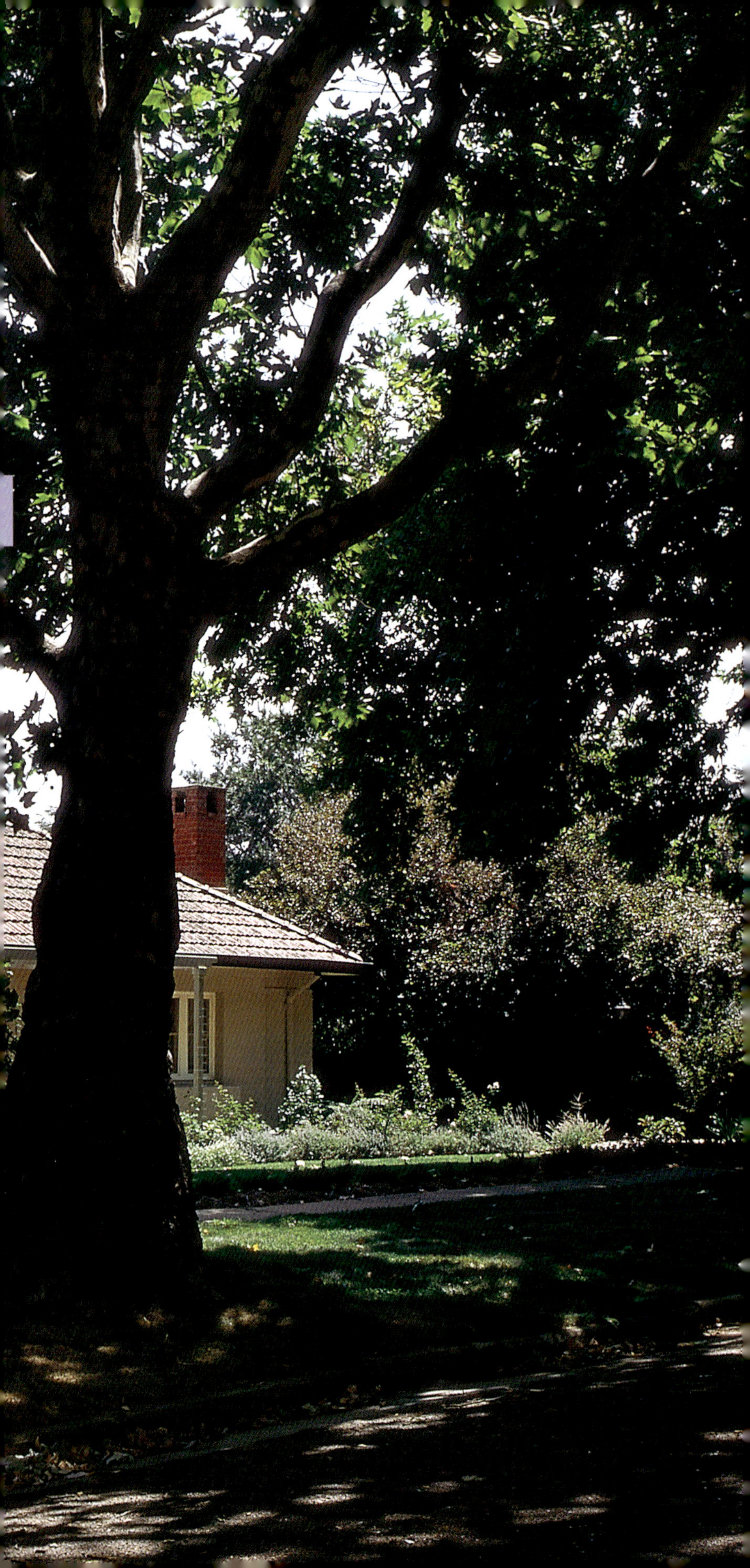

Inner North

*T*he Inner North, that part of Canberra immediately to the north of Lake Burley Griffin, Civic and the ANU is also bounded by the Canberra Nature Park to the east, west and north. This area, which also includes the Australian Defence Force Academy [ADFA], the Royal Military College, Duntroon and Pialligo, also contains large parts of the city's built heritage from the pre National Capital era, all connected to the Campbell family's 19th century pastoral property 'Duntroon'.

The suburbs of Ainslie and Reid were amongst the earliest parts of Canberra to be developed. For visitors in the early 1930s they would have marked the edge of the city, or town as it really was then. Campbell, favoured initially by the military, dates from the early 1960s and contains five houses by Roy Grounds. By around 1970 the supply of suburban blocks was almost exhausted all through the inner north, so the whole area fits more-or-less into a development cycle of four decades.

Towards the beginning of the current century, a new wave of greater density development came to the Inner North, particularly in Braddon which became a zone of townhouses and apartments in the process. Through its being a major city entry route, the Northbourne Avenue corridor is a special case and development is guided by the National Capital Authority's vision for a uniform 25 metre height limit. At the southern end of Northbourne Avenue, where groups of eight storey buildings are starting to form, an impression of the eventual impact of this policy may be seen.

Opposite: Reid Urban Conservation Area

38 Duntroon House

Harrison Road, Royal Military College, Duntroon
1862 Campbell family
GC, V, NA

Built for Robert Campbell [d 1846], who established a 4,000 acre property here in the mid-1820s, Duntroon House is a significant example of a major limestone plains pastoral homestead. Campbell also operated warehouses in Sydney and his rural estate was expanded with further grants in 1827, 1830 and 1832. Originally known as Pialligo, his holdings grew to include other structures such as the Duntroon Dairy [near Russell], Blundells Cottage [now in Kings Park], St John's Church and School [Reid], plantings in Glebe Park [Civic] as well as the Mugga Mugga and Majura homesteads.

Duntroon was built in two major stages. The first, called 'Limestone Cottage', a single storey Georgian building with a veranda on three sides, was commenced in 1833 before Robert Campbell moved from Sydney. The second stage was undertaken in 1862 by Robert's third son George and his wife Marianne. Researchers believe they were assisted by Alberto Dias Soares, a former architect/engineer who arrived in the district as an Anglican Minister in 1862. This latter work resulted in a two storey stone dwelling of substance designed in the fashionable Gothic Revival style of the period. George and Marianne also took the opportunity to 'gothicise' the smaller Limestone Cottage – in the veranda column treatment for example – probably around the same time.

After George Campbell died in England in 1881 Marianne returned and lived in Duntroon House until her own death in 1903. Then the house remained vacant until the Royal Military College was established on the Campbell estate in 1910 and the homestead was renovated as offices for senior ranks and single quarters for officers. Duntroon House is now the Officers Mess and remains a pivotal landmark in a much-enlarged RMC campus.

The original Limestone Cottage

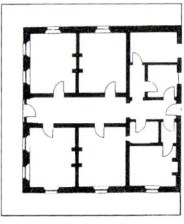

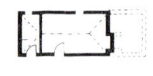

Floor plan with separate kitchen and scullery (broken line), Stage 1 c1833

Inner North

39 Anzac Memorial Chapel of St Paul
Miles Road, Royal Military College, Duntroon
1966 Fowell Mansfield and MacLurcan
GC, V, NA

The Royal Military College's Anzac Memorial Chapel (seen here from the rear) is a fine example from the ecclesiastical work of the Sydney architectural practice Fowell Mansfield and MacLurcan. Apart from its RMC role, the site is also the headquarters for a chaplaincy.

There are two chapels here representing in fact the categories that exist in the national Christian religion: one, seating 550, for Anglican and Protestant denominations and the other, seating 350 for the Roman Catholics. The building plan accommodates this duality by providing a tall, hexagonal-shaped narthex entry space between the chapels to serve as a common entry point. The two chapels 'plug' into either side of this top-lit narthex and form a wing-shaped plan. The chapel complex was constructed by the Royal Military Engineers in a little over 12 months and dedicated in May 1966. Except for the addition of a small meeting room in 1986, it remains as built.

With its white-painted brick walls, dark tiled roofs and extensive use of natural timber in ceilings, floors and joinery the Anzac Memorial Chapel is a well-mannered example of the circumspect 1960s 'Sydney School' architectural aesthetic that, retrospectively, appears genteel, but was keener in its own time.

Only a short distance to the left of the entrance to the Anzac Memorial Chapel is another much smaller chapel whose sides are open to the elements. This is the Changi Chapel, originally constructed by Australian prisoners of war in Changi camp, Singapore in 1944. The small building was brought to Australia at the end of the Second World War and is now the National Prisoner-of-War memorial.

The road behind the Anzac Memorial Chapel leads on to General Bridges Drive which in turn goes to the summit of Mount Pleasant. On its way it passes the grave of Major-General Sir William Throsby Bridges, the first Commandant of the Royal Military College, Duntroon.

The memorial stone on this grave is the only structure in Canberra built to Walter Burley Griffin's design. Typically, the low slab of dark stone is in harmony with the bushland setting.

Changi Chapel, RMC Duntroon

40 Grandstand and Amenities Building
Oval 1 [beside Main Parade Ground], Australian Defence Force Academy, Campbell
1984 Bruce Bowden [Department of Housing and Construction]
GC, V, NA

This simple little work of architecture appeared amongst the flurry of construction that accompanied the rapid ADFA construction program of the early to middle 1980s. It is embedded into, but rises above, the earth bank that separates the Academy's Oval No 1 from the Main Parade Ground. It is no more than a stepped seating area with a flat roof suspended from pairs of circular steel masts. On a terrace level at the top of the seating, a free-standing glass block wall screens the seating area from the Parade Ground and the prevailing westerly wind. Underneath the seating, buried in the bank, there are change rooms and amenities. These are top lit from light shafts originating at the base of the glass block wall.

Simply conceived and rigorously executed, this building has all the clarity of a conceptual diagram and much of the élan that comes from carefully making an aesthetic statement out of structure and construction.

41 Capital Jet Facility
Boomerang Street, Canberra Airport
1998 Daryl Jackson, Alastair Swayn
GC, V, NA

This appropriately sleek and slipstreamed building is a private aviation facility built for the airport's owner Terry Snow. Its modular design deploys a cube form for the aircraft hanger and then, attached to that, an elliptical cylinder is used for the associated office and administration functions.

These elements, combined with the use of finely crafted exterior metal cladding and bold, horizontal fenestration, situate the design fairly and squarely in the 20th century architectural tradition generally referred to as Functionalism in which all architectural elements from the building's plan to its forms and details, are processed in the act of design according to a utilitarian ethic much in the way that an aeroplane needs to be. Arguably, few building types are as well suited to this architectural approach as buildings for air transport are.

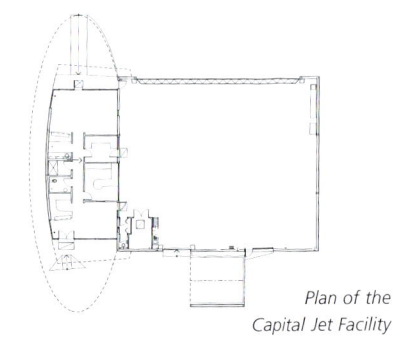

Plan of the Capital Jet Facility

Q15

42 Three Houses
42 (pictured), 44 and 46 Vasey Crescent, Campbell
1961 Roy Grounds [Grounds Romberg and Boyd]
GC, V, NA

These three houses were built on the edge of a nature reserve in the new suburb of Campbell as a co-ordinated group for three owners, two of whom were from Melbourne and familiar with the architect's work. Each house is different, no doubt as different as the clients were in their detail requirements, but given a common denominator by the site planning on this hilly street with views to Mt. Ainslie and Lake Burley Griffin. Grounds staggered the site position of the three houses so that they shared the view corridor. This meant that No. 42, the Philip House, was set the farthest back from the street, had the lowest site level and was two stories, the Griffing House, No. 44 is in the middle and No. 46, the Blakers House is highest up the hill and closest to the street.

All three houses are designed in section so that parking is underneath and the ground floor of each of the houses is built at the same level. All have a three-storey format with clearly demarcated zones for parents and children, and yet they are all different. But they are of simple form, made from everyday materials and convey modesty with economical and rational design and construction clearly evident. Architecturally the houses are all variants on the Melbourne Regionalist theme, which is a trait they share with the other Grounds houses on the other side of Campbell and works elsewhere in Canberra. Incidentally, Robin Boyd managed the construction stage of work after Grounds accepted the Victorian Arts Centre commission.

Today the Vasey Crescent Group is almost totally surrounded by a substrate of mature native landscaping that provides good screening from the street. Over time No. 44 has been the most altered [1973, 1976 and 1990], but the other two residences have stayed within the original families and are little changed.

Visitors to Canberra frequently lose their way even when going relatively short distances. This city does not have a straight grid pattern of streets like most, and newcomers do not realise the extent they have turned when proceeding along a gently curving circuit or crescent. Loops and flyovers can also take the unwary motorist to a seemingly far-distant and impromptu destination from the one intended. However by using a few major landmarks such as the flagstaff of Parliament House or the Telstra tower on Black Mountain as constants, much of this can be avoided. An aerial view, such as the one on the endpapers of this guide is a useful tool and when used in conjunction with a map will clarify problems of orientation.

43 Housing [medium density]
Blamey Crescent and Edmondson Street, Campbell
1968 Harry Seidler
GC, V, NA

Essentially a large 42 unit apartment house surrounded by a 'curtilage' of seven separate terraces of townhouses containing another 32 dwellings, this notable housing scheme is one of two built by the Australian National University in the mid 1960s and is the only one left standing, although no longer a university property. In Campbell the trademark Seidler efficiency in site and building planning has accommodated 74 dwellings on a 4 acre site without it seeming at all overcrowded or diminished in amenity.

Capitalising on a gradual slope up from the street he has employed split-level sectional design to get most parking into building fronts from below and then located the first level of accommodation half a level up and behind. By systematic arrangement of building elements and devices such as opposing skillion roof slopes, skylights, expression of party walls, sun-shading, in-board balconies, concrete block screens, sheet metal spandrels and garden walls, Seidler has created a great deal of variety in architectural form. By contrast there is a radical limitation on the number of different materials used: yellow-cream face brick, white metal sheeting and roofing and not much else.

The ANU eventually sold the Campbell dwellings to individuals and it is now operated by a body corporate and this has been its salvation. On the other hand the University retained ownership of the second, a 104-dwelling development in Garran, but by the end of the century these too were sold off and redeveloped to finance capital works on the main campus.

44 House
11 Waller Crescent Campbell
c1968 Neville Ward
GC, V, NA

Ward, who had worked with Malcolm Moir, produced other houses in Canberra [one at 212 Dryandra Street, O'Connor for example], but none as successful as this house, which is unusual for its use of a large central courtyard in its plan. Designed for a ridge-top site with westerly views, the major courtyard is like an outdoor room: it is appropriately dimensioned for sun penetration and accessible from all sides and, at the rear, from two storeys of accommodation.

As you look across the courtyard to more of the same building on the other side it gives the house a great sense of diversity but also privacy, both from the street and from one part of it to any other. The courtyard strategy combined with Modernist traits such as flat roofs, cantilevers, timber joinery of dark hues and naturalistic landscaping all coalesce to produce a sort of Japanese character.

45 House
2 Ryrie Street, Campbell
c1965 Anon
GC, V, NA

This relatively unknown house in a corner of Campbell near the War Memorial is the work of an unknown designer. Its architectural lineage seems to include the Breueresque aspects of Harry Seidler's residential architecture. At Ryrie Street we find the use of refined materials in stark contrast to natural ones – render versus stone walling for example and the notion of a courtyard space recessed into the building mass but conceived as an outdoor room and shielded by vertical louvres for another.

No. 2 Ryrie Street uses the bi-polar plan separating the house into zones, or pavilions: there is a rectangular pavilion with its long side facing northwards to the street and an offset one behind it for bedrooms. In between are the 'utility spaces' essentially the kitchen, which joins the two pavilions together. The roof slopes gently down the site from the street, with the tallest volume over the Living Room. This roof is carried right across the frontage of the block to make a carport held up on a blade wall one of the interesting features of the house.

46 Two Houses
4 [pictured] and 24 Cobby Street, Campbell
1964 and 1970 Roy Grounds
[Grounds Romberg and Boyd]
GC, V, NA

These two houses are situated at opposite ends of the same street. Backing on to the Nature Park and Mount Ainslie, internally they both have virtually intact interiors with a comprehensive use of Tasmanian Oak timber ceilings and joinery and they both have a flow of space from living rooms to protected exterior courtyards.

No. 24, at the west end of Cobby Street, is a rectangular, two storey, brick L shaped plan house with a walled courtyard space contiguous with the living and dining spaces inside. The single story No. 4, built for the émigré scientist Otto Frankel, is less conventional with its long, thin, slightly curved floor plan. It presents a rather forbidding brick wall to the street, but opens up beautifully to the garden, which has a similar partly walled courtyard space connected to the living areas. Although this house wasn't built until 1970, it was designed in the 1960s. However, for this period, it seems the more radical of these two interesting Grounds houses.

47 St John's Church and Schoolhouse
1 Anzac Parade West, Reid
1845–78 George Campbell, Alberto Soares and Edmund Blacket
GC, V, A

St John's Church dates from the period of early European settlement when Robert Campbell, the patriarch of Duntroon, oversaw completion of the Schoolhouse and the bluestone nave of the church a year before he died in 1846. At this time it served the people of Duntroon and district. The next significant building stage came almost three decades later in the 1870s when Alberto Soares, who had assisted Robert's son George with major additions to Duntroon in 1862, finished a sandstone chancel in 1872. By 1880 the church was substantially finished with the construction of the Edmund Blacket designed tower [1868] and the spire [1878].

St Johns is used by the British Royal family during state visits and has been associated with Governors General, particularly Viscount D'Lisle who donated bells to the church in memory of his wife and Viscount Dunrossil who, in 1961, died in office and was buried in the churchyard. Both the church and the school have important associations with early settlement of Canberra and were formerly isolated buildings in a rural Australian pastoral setting. Their present context stands in stark relief to that of their early years: at the time of the competition for the design of Canberra they were depicted surrounded by paddocks and trees on their own.

48 Reid Urban Conservation Area
Anzac Parade, Limestone Avenue, Coranderrk and Booroondara Streets
1925–30 Federal Capital Commission
GC, V, A

An area of about 70 hectares abutting Civic, this complex of streets, squares, public gardens, pedestrian walkways, mature verge trees and many houses in original mid to late twenties condition, is a fine example of an Australianised English Garden Suburb design. Executed with a civic benevolence once considered normal for government as developer, the network of streets and spaces focuses on Dirrawan and Geerilong Gardens, which are of a size roughly equal to the smallest Georgian square in London, but enclosed by cottages rather than a wall of low-rise residences.

The houses divulge a catalogue of fashion with influences from sources as disparate as Arts and Crafts, Georgian cottage and Mediterranean styles. Individually no one thing stands out, but as a whole, particularly with a dominance of white and off-white painted render, this part of Reid has a consistency that is estimable.

49 Housing medium density [Jerilderie Court]
Ainslie Avenue, Doonkuna, Allambee and Elimatta Streets, Reid
1977 Philip Cox
GC, V, NA

Philip Cox's conceptual response to the NCDC brief for a total of 62 public housing units on a single block in Reid was to create two rows of accommodation comprising townhouses facing Ainslie Avenue and flats facing Allambee street with car parking restricted to the underside of the apartments. The semi-private space between is pedestrian and communal – and, significantly, it is the address and entry point for all dwellings.

In order to have them facing due north for solar access, all the buildings are turned at 45 degrees to the street, a stratagem that the NCDC client resisted for some time before finally accepting. They then extended the idea as a design control in the adjoining private developments. Cox's architecture at Jerilderie Court can be seen as vertically layered – obviously accommodation is layered in the apartment block, but so too are all the building elevations which change materials as they rise from the ground and there is a pronounced three-dimensional planar effect of the repeating blade walls moving through the site.

Through its measured use of well-proven ideas about layout, address and privacy, Jerilderie Court is one of the more successful medium density schemes in Canberra, particularly compared to nearby slab block and high-rise examples. Unfortunately, fine examples of original detailing like the 'flower-pot' balcony balustrades was lost in 2000 when they were removed and replaced, insensitively, with crude metal models. That apart, the project continues to be well maintained and cared for not just by the ACT Government, but by the residents as well.

The high point behind the Australian War Memorial is Mount Ainslie – the perfect spot from which the visitor may take his or her bearings on the whole Canberra region. Looking south a panoramic view is afforded down Anzac Parade, across Lake Burley Griffin to Parliament House and on to the Brindabella Ranges in the distance – the Blue Hills of Gwen Meredith's epic ABC radio serial of the past set in the countryside around Canberra.

50 Ainslie Fire Station
Wakefield Avenue [at Limestone Avenue] Ainslie
1993 Hal Guida [Mitchell Giurgola Thorp]
GC, V, NA

'I suspect that any architect would love to design a fire station. For one thing there is the chance to be a child again. A fire station encompasses a synthesis of movement and staticity, and the tension of something that must suddenly bounce with a roaring movement is implied' [Romaldo Giurgola, 1996 UME 1]

Indeed, fire stations are emblematical, they embody the dual ideas of public service through their personnel and technology through the equipment housed. Ainslie Fire station connects amply with this tradition. Its architecture is constructed from two masonry boxes either side of a wide open, glassy engine room, the whole assemblage surmounted by a metal roof that has the visual weightlessness of an aeroplane wing.

Facing north to Wakefield Avenue the eastern brick pavilion is essentially for staff daytime functions and the western one for nightime use. The engine room is the connecting piece, its architectural form of light steel framing and glass infill is, appropriately, the antithesis of the adjoining brick forms.

51 Houses
Alt Crescent Group 6 and 8 Alt Crescent, Ainslie
1930 Federal Capital Commission
GC, V, NA

These two houses are the most architecturally intact part of a tree-lined crescent of dwellings facing Limestone Avenue not far from the intersection with Ainslie Avenue. They were built between 1925 and 1930 by the Federal Capital Commission [FCC] through the agency of their Chief Architect H Rolland for the use of middle-income public servants who were scheduled to move to Canberra in the first big wave of relocations that accompanied the moving of Parliament to Canberra in 1927. Rolland's office designed twenty-two different house types for the FCC and five of them appear in Alt Crescent. In their planned setting they exemplify the post-1920 Garden City architectural and planning ideas that took root in Canberra after the departure of – and in partial distinction to – Walter Burley and Marion Mahoney Griffin with their different ideas about residential architecture and planning.

Derived from a mixture of the elegiac English cottage tradition and Edwardian Arts and Crafts architectural tendencies, the Alt Crescent group are early period government houses intended for upper-middle management. The original lessees included many of the FCC's own senior staff and a police constable who became Commissioner. Eventually all government housing in Canberra became known colloquially as 'guvies' – so in Canberra parlance, these are early guvies. The suite of Garden City planning ideas used here includes variegated house setbacks from the street, no front fences, a mix of house types and landscaped public space. Along Limestone Avenue there is Arizona Cypress street planting and Roman Cypress plantings in the crescent itself.

N13

52 Ainslie Public School
[Infants School]
30 Doonkuna Street, Braddon
1927 JS Murdoch
GC, V, A

Opened in 1927, four months after Parliament, Ainslie Public School's significance is more social and historical than architectural being the second school built in the capital. It is now used as a Secondary Introductory English Centre.

Attributed to John Smith Murdoch, the architect for Provisional Parliament House, the single-storey school building had an H-shaped symmetrical plan of classrooms and support facilities. It was enlarged in the 1940s and the early1950s and its architectural style is the conservative stripped Classicism [or tentative Modernism] of the day, deploying rendered and painted brickwork, some contemporary interpretation of classical decoration, an axial portico fed by a semi-circular driveway and a pitched roof partly concealed behind parapet walls. The regular pattern of large glass windows is interesting and may reveal the Department of Works and Railways architectural staff were conscious of the 1920s fashion for sunlight and fresh air that is evident in places as diverse as California and Berlin at the same time.

The adjoining Art Deco style Ainslie Primary School, designed by departmental architects EH Henderson and Cuthbert Whitley, was opened in 1938. The Ainslie site constitutes an important remnant of public education in early Canberra.

Ainslie Primary School designed by EH Henderson and Cuthbert Whitley

54

N12

54 Two Houses [Whitley Houses]
107 Limestone Avenue [pictured above] and 65 Torrens Street, Braddon
1940 Cuthbert Whitley [Department of Interior Works Branch]
GC, V, NA

The Limestone Avenue house is one of five extant between-the-wars modernist government houses in Canberra designed by the senior departmental architect Cuthbert Whitley [1886–1942]. They were designed and built during 1939–40 in a flurry of departmental events surrounding the death of Chief Architect Edwin Henderson in June 1939, the declaration of war in September and the removal of the whole Department of Interior Works Branch to Melbourne in November. Whitley, who joined the Department in 1912, and had been mentored by JS Murdoch, moved to Canberra permanently in 1929 to run the Department of Works and Railways' architectural office under Henderson. He is credited with the major design role in Ainslie Primary School and in Canberra High School [now the School of Art] and acted in the Chief Architect position between June and November of 1939.

Whitley's interest in European architectural modernism seems to have been shared by Henderson himself as the Department's work in the 1930s shows a drift away from 1920s Canberra Anglo influences to the Stripped Classicism and Art Deco of the schools in Ainslie and Acton. Later on these influences extended to government houses which display an awareness of developments such as the Bauhaus, the Stuttgart and Vienna housing exhibitions and the MoMA 'International Style' exhibition of 1932.

The other Whitley pre-war house at 65 Torrens Street in Braddon has been altered by an addition and the windows have been replaced. Nonetheless it is still worthy of consideration. There are also three Whitley houses in Griffith – see 'Inner South'.

The two Whitley houses in Braddon are interesting in that they were designed in face brick, to be left unpainted. The Limestone Avenue house is in an intact condition and gives a glimpse of the progressive architectural vision that was extant here at the beginning of the Second World War, and didn't re-surface until much later.

55 National Seventh Day Adventist Church
3 Macleay Street, Turner
1971 Ken Woolley [Ancher Mortlock Murray and Woolley]
GC, V, A

A dramatic statement wrought from a 45 degree brick prism and the formation of a courtyard are the ideas that underpin this church complex in Turner. Ken Woolley retained an existing church building on the site as a new hall and added two new wings to it to form a U shaped courtyard. A low-scaled one, housing educational and youth facilities, is at right angles to the existing hall and the high prism itself is parallel to it.

Inside the nave, in spite of expectations, the congregation doesn't face the dominant spatial direction of the prism, but sits at right angles to it. There is a noticeable spareness about the interior with few conventional religious icons, not even a cross on display. The church is intended to be a community meeting place. The focus therefore is on the congregation. The Seventh Day Adventist emphasis on the rite of baptism is picked up neatly in the large reflecting pool, which runs down one side of the nave and reflects light into the interior.

56 Holy Trinity Lutheran National Memorial Church
22 Watson Street, Turner
1961 Grounds Romberg and Boyd
GC, V, A

This church by Grounds Romberg and Boyd is a paradigm of simplicity. A plan the shape of a square has its east and west sides filled in with ancillary accommodation. The remaining floor space – including all four corners – is left open. The entry is then positioned at the south end and the altar at the north. A pyramid roof and tower with skylight finish it all off.

The square theme extends further with the nave occupying a square within the first square and the broken pyramid shaped roof nestling comfortably over the whole thing with a generous overhang all round to form veranda spaces on all four sides. Some have called the interior one of the best in Canberra, certainly, with its mountain ash ceiling, windows and doors and the stack bonded concrete masonry wall detail, it is one of the most interesting.

57 Housing [medium density]
Northbourne Housing Precinct

Northbourne Avenue, Morphett Street and Wakefield Avenue, Lyneham and Dickson
1962 Ancher Mortlock and Murray
GC, V, NA

Sydney Ancher [1904–79] was an enthusiast for European Modern Architecture. No doubt when he was touring the continent as a young architect in the early 1930s – he is known to have visited the Berlin Building Exhibition of 1932 for example – he was at his most receptive to its aesthetic and social applications. Back in Australia Ancher worked to find receptive ground for this Modernism in the Australian cultural, climatic and technological environment of the late 1930s and afterwards in the 50s and 60s. One of the fruits of that labour, the Northbourne Housing Precinct – won in a limited competition – is the most, possibly the only, significant public housing scheme Ancher produced.

Working with planner Denis Winston, Ancher crafted a new gateway for Canberra on Northbourne Avenue with a development of 169 dwelling units sited on both sides of the street. It was an ambitious undertaking and one that has entered the annals of regional architectural history. For years, Ancher's project has distracted followers of architecture who have driven into the city and felt the frisson of imagining themselves inside a 1930s German or Austrian Seidlung. However, for most people this is probably way too arcane.

The mix of types and modes is extensive: there are 77 three bed units, 36 two bed units, 28 one bed units and 28 bedsitters distributed in five different block types – four storey bedsitter blocks, two storey pair houses, three storey maisonettes, single storey courtyard flats and three storey flats. Describing the project site planning strategy Ancher said 'Building blocks have been arranged in various housing types to make a formal pattern to Northbourne Avenue with rear entries. This provides common spaces and other open spaces between buildings'. Thus there were no vehicular movements on the site proper, only pedestrian flows from those rear entries.

Although they are small and built to a budget, the various blocks taken together do represent a consistent vision of Canberra public housing at mid century with a generous provision of open space and some limited balcony and terrace spaces for the occupiers, a restrained, modernist architectural vocabulary incorporating flat roofs, prismatic massing and understated details. Unfortunately, this very brave scheme, which tried a plethora of interesting ideas and social combinations with bags of potential spin-off, was the only such scheme Ancher executed in the capital and the experience gained here was not re-invested.

58 Dickson Library
Dickson Place, Dickson
1964 Enrico Taglietti
GC, V, A

The Dickson Library was the first district library constructed in Canberra and it is the first building of Taglietti's that confirmed the emergence of his own distinctive architectural style after his work on the Italian Embassy. The original brief was for a library of 30,000 volumes with a children's area containing 10,000 books.

The elements of Taglietti's emergent style at Dickson that appeared in later projects include the sheltering external wall designed with abstract openings, clerestory lighting, the deep horizontal fascia 'floating' over – and cantilevering past – support walls, visual buttressing of the corners with half pylons, the use of corner courtyards and the decorative use of rainwater systems. What is different about the Dickson Library is the absolute symmetry – in plan, section and elevation. Although the symmetry isn't related to Classical models, and it isn't overt at Dickson, Taglietti dropped it in subsequent projects and in fact made asymmetry a standard point of departure for most of his work.

In 1997 the Dickson Library was altered slightly, with Taglietti's involvement, to install automatic doors and an after hours return chute. Otherwise it is operating much as it has since it was opened.

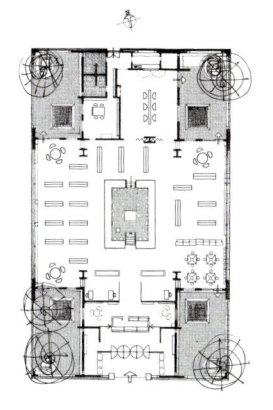

Plan of Dickson Library

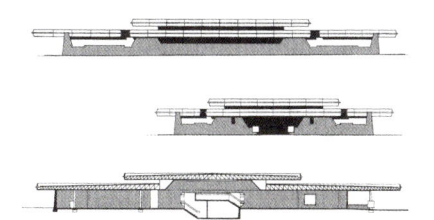

Top: West elevation
Middle: South elevation
Bottom: Longitudinal section

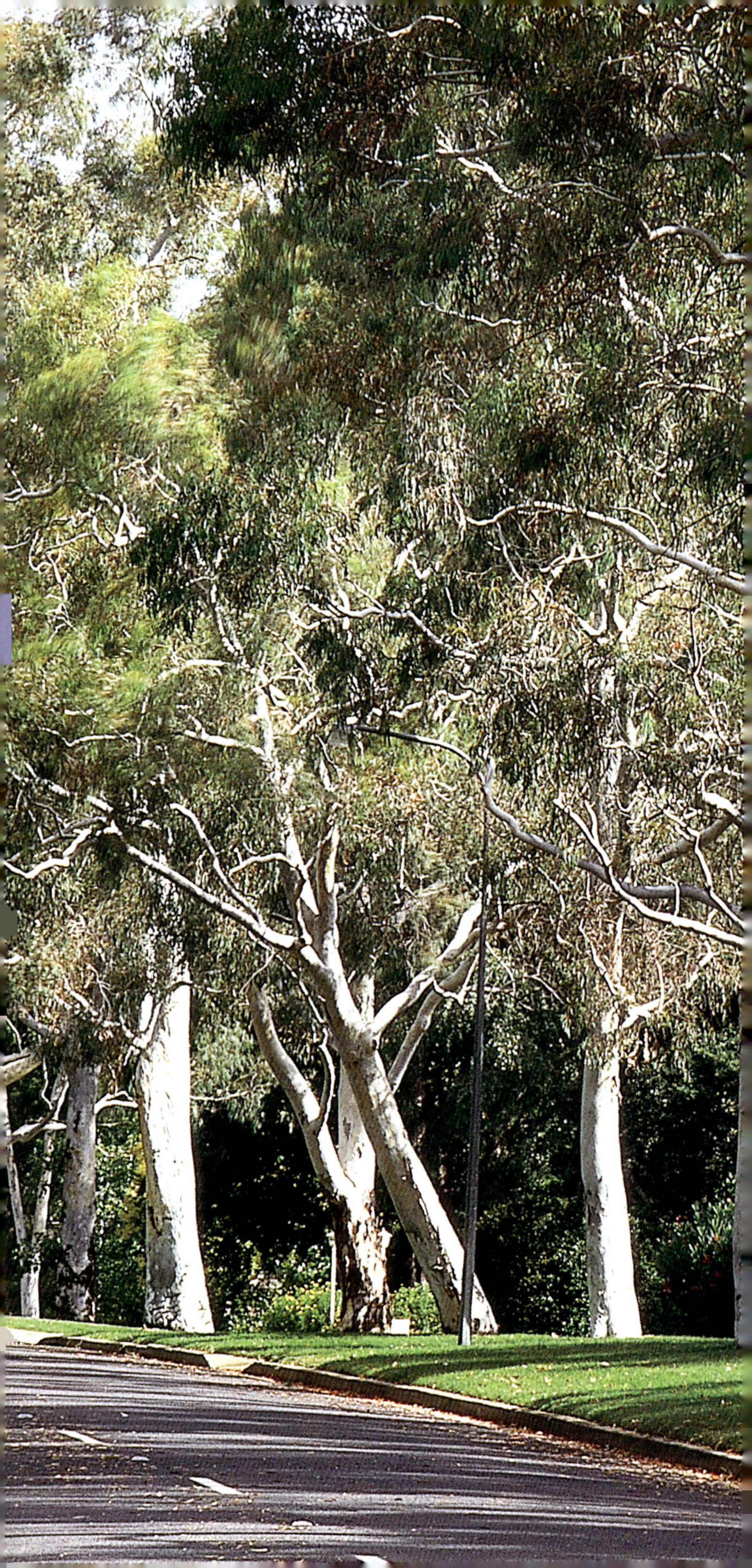

Inner South

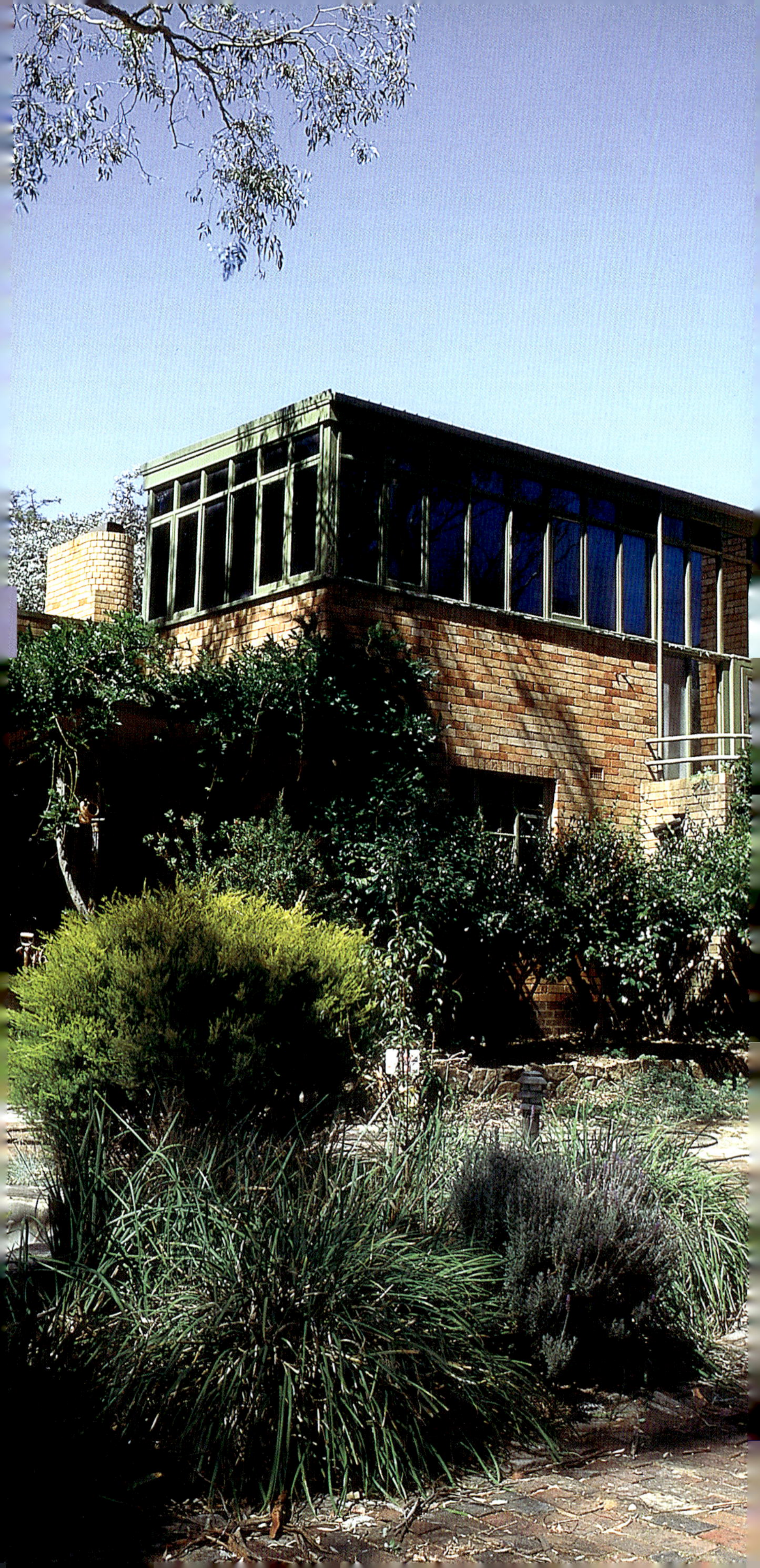

Inner South

The Inner South comprises the first grouping of suburbs abutting the southern edge of Lake Burley Griffin and the Parliamentary Zone. In 1913 a Departmental Board prepared an implementation version of Walter Burley Griffin's plan for Canberra [without the competition winner's knowledge], then designated this area the 'Initial City.' This move reflects its proximity to the proposed Capitol Hill grouping and the railway station. Climatically it is also a part of inner Canberra nicely sheltered from the pitiless westerlies that blow through the city, particularly in winter. Even though the Griffins subsequent arrival in Australia headed off many of the Department's transgressions, this one, probably though being mild compared to some others, survived. Thus the Inner South became home to the higher echelon public servants, the early retail centres of Manuka and Kingston and the elite private schools. It also accommodated most of the 'cathedral' sites when they were distributed by the Federal Government in the 1920s.

Today the area, which includes the suburbs of Yarralumla, Deakin, Griffith, Red Hill, Narradundah and Kingston, is probably the part of Canberra where interesting architecture is thickest on the ground, including works by Seidler, Grounds, Boyd, Moir, Bolt, Cox, Jelinek, Woolley, Desbrowe-Annear, Whitley and Taglietti. The area also contains most of the embassies and a significant number of churches, including Canberra's only Cathedral and the Apostolic Nunciature.

The Inner South tends to have the highest value residential real estate in the whole of Canberra. Like the Inner North, residential redevelopment pressure is felt here, although it happened earlier here with Kingston accommodating much of the town houses, apartments and even high rise residential towers. In the early decades of the 21st century the Kingston foreshore site is likely to be the place of even more new medium and higher density residential development.

59

59 Embassy–Sweden
[Royal Swedish Legation]
5 Turrana Street, Yarralumla
1951 EGH Lundquist and Peddle,
Thorp & Walker
GC, V, NA

The Swedish Embassy building was designed by the Swede EGH Lundquist in 1947 perhaps with the idea of ensuring an emblematic Swedish building was erected as one of Canberra's first diplomatic headquarters. The Swedish architect's design work was developed and documented by Sydney architects Peddle Thorp and Walker who also site managed the project through to its completion in 1951. This conservative, elegiac architectural statement won the Sulman Award in 1952, the first of four Sulmans for Canberra in the 1950s.

Set in a commanding position overlooking extensive grounds, the long rectangular two-storey building contains offices and an Ambassador's residence at opposite ends. Photography falls short of capturing its understated ease produced with simple white painted bagged brick forms and a basic rhythm of window openings all set underneath a wide projecting eaves and an almost flat copper roof. A caretaker's residence and garage complete the grouping, which today looks much as it did when first built, except that the landscape planting has matured.

60 Embassy–Japan
112 Empire Circuit, Yarralumla
c1965 T Sakamaki in association with
Grounds Romberg and Boyd
GC, V, NA

If expression of structure is a recurring theme in post-war Modern architecture, so it is for Japanese architecture, both traditional and modern. In their corner-sited Japanese Embassy, Grounds Romberg and Boyd blended both these traditions together with the starkly plain black on white aesthetic that if often seen in traditional Japanese architecture.

The whole two-storey embassy edifice is a spare and restrained outing for the Melbourne firm who were doing a lot of work in Canberra at the time. This is so especially for Grounds, who seems to have preferred working with an expression of walls and roof rather than structural framing – witness the two houses in Cobby Street, Campbell for example.

In 2003 substantial restorations to the Chancery building were commenced.

It's notable that Robin Boyd, a member of the practice, had a pervasive interest in modern Japanese architecture that eventually found an outlet in his books Kenzo Tange *[1962] and* New Directions In Japanese Architecture *[1968].*

61 Embassy–Switzerland

7 Melbourne Avenue, Forrest
1975 Hermann and Hans Peter Baur
GC, V, NA

Arguably, Hermann and Hans Peter Baur's sober, yet beautiful Swiss diplomatic premises represent that country's modern architecture as tellingly as any Canberra embassy does for it's national architecture except perhaps for the Mexican and the Finnish complexes in nearby Yarralumla.

Set on the high ground of a large, wooded corner site, the Baur's work deploys the Swiss modernist canon with cubic forms, flat roofs, simple brick facades, a rectangular plan and a partly free-standing, west-facing concrete brise-soleil stretching right across the street elevation.

Throughout his long career Hermann Baur [1894–1980] rehearsed and developed an architecture of spareness rather than splendour. Based predominantly in Basel his reputation was gained from works in housing, educational buildings, hospitals, but perhaps most of all churches – he designed more than thirty. The Canberra project came towards the end of his life and it is likely that his son Hans Peter [b1922], was the significant player. Peter Baur was still practising in Basel at the turn of the century.

62 Embassy–Ireland

20 Arkana Street, Yarralumla
1981 Philip Cox
GC, V, NA

It's palpable that the traditional rural building complex, with its play of white washed walls and steep, thatched roofs, is an extreme cliché of Irish-ness. That Philip Cox was aware of it is also obvious. In the design of this elegant L-shaped building then, it is an achievement that he has referred so freely to without actually falling victim to its pitfalls. Somehow, by alluding to Australian vernacular traditions as well as manipulating the form palette of white walls, chimneys and grey green roof and including the variation of separate garden walls as well, Cox has turned the cliché into a trope. This project has all the visual simplicity and even quietude of a farm compound, but it is a working embassy with office, reception and residential activities in it.

In his early career Cox was highly attuned to the aesthetic parallels between vernacular building and contemporary architecture. It's a theme that attracted many others and it is one of the enduring counter themes of modern architectural history. Cox's early achievements with Ian McKay at Tocal and Leppington colleges in NSW, and his book *Rude Timber Buildings in Australia* are other manifestations of this interest. As his practice evolved however, other thematic material, better suited to the design of large buildings, took over.

63 Embassy–Mexico
14 Perth Avenue, Yarralumla
1982 Terrazas de la Pena
[with Anthony Cooper]
GC, V, A

De la Pena's clear and effortless mastery of primary architectural forms such as walls and roof is a salient feature of this embassy. The concept of the ever-present roof hovering over the site and the use of solid walls discreetly recessed underneath it and beside it is most graceful. The site itself slopes to the north in the direction of the lake and is big enough to allow two similar but slightly different buildings: one for chancery and the other for residential functions. Appropriately the chancery, at the top of the sloping site, is grander in scale than the residence lower down.

The careful control of fenestration to exclude windows on all but the north facades and the remarkable roof form largely determines the architectural outcome at the Mexican Embassy. The effect of this strategy is sublimely illustrated at the entry off Perth Avenue where a freestanding wall as high as a tower guides the visitor towards the blank entry façade interrupted only by a pair of glass entry doors. Once inside the interiors, with their cave-like enclosure of surrounding walls, open up generously with full glazing to the north and onwards to terraces and gardens.

64 Embassy–Finland
120 Darwin Avenue, Yarralumla
2001 Hirvonen-Huttenen and MGT
GC, V, NA

This solid glass and concrete prism is a major extension to the original Finnish Embassy next door [Rommel Moorcroft, 1978]. It accommodates a full compliment of embassy functions and one residential apartment in its elongated three storey high glass and concrete form. Outside there is a formal entry courtyard on one side and a more informal garden with a sauna on the other.

As these exterior forms make an elegant and refined statement in glass and metal wall construction, the building and its natural setting explores the dialectic of nature and culture rather well – the natural appears more so because of the highly technical building and vice versa. The building's interior presents itself as a world of natural light amongst a variety of warm timber surfaces in floors, wall panelling and joinery.

At the outset of the 21st century this building presents a vision of the architectural future through Finnish lenses, and it thus takes its place beside other recent Finnish Embassy constructions, most notably the 1993 Washington Embassy by Heikkinen and Komonen for example.

L16

65 Town houses [Lakeview Townhouses]
127 Hopetoun Circuit, Yarralumla
1984 Harry Seidler
GC, V, NA

In the trajectory of Harry Seidler's architecture this group of 11 identical three-bedroom townhouses contains some established Seidleresque design motifs and some newer ones as well. The outside forms with expressed party walls, metal pitched roofs and north facing balconies are little different to the equivalent houses in the Campbell group of 20 years earlier, but the fan shaped site plan and the Rococco play of curves in the interior of the dwellings are ample evidence of the architect's late career interest in non-orthogonal geometries that determined the exterior form of his Horizon Apartments [1997] in Sydney for example.

The site plan has the 11 townhouses fanning out to the north and the lake view from an entry garden court, which is actually the roof of an underground garage. Here also there are curvilinear cut-outs in the court floor to allow ingress of natural light and ventilation to the garage, and there are private courtyards that moderate the privacy switch at the entry to each unit. The houses are split level with central stairs; ground floor living rooms and first floor master bedrooms occupy the north façade leaving kitchens and tertiary bedrooms to the south. The centre of the plan opens up with a rising stair and dining room at the bottom of a double height volume. This central space is the site of the interplay of curved balustrading moving from one planimetric curvature to the opposite on different levels.

L16

66 Clynes House
1 Fitzgerald Street, Yarralumla
2001 Rodney Moss [Cox Humphries Moss]
GC, V, NA

This corner house on the edge of a diplomatic zone is a thoughtful rendering of the elusive, archetypal 'Canberra House' that is talked about locally but rarely defined. Some of the best Canberra residential architecture has emerged from a mixture of diverse ingredients including climate, early 20th century Garden City house styles and post war Modernist residential architecture – especially Swedish and Finnish models.

Accepting this important tradition, the Clynes House is an object lesson in clarity using clearly defined pavilions to separate and characterise living and sleeping domains. The house seems to exude serenity and liveability. The design and detailing task has been carefully executed with an exemplary level of refinement and appropriate restraint. The result is an essay in simplicity that again proves the old adage that architecture is often as much about what is left out as what is put in. For its place in time it is something of an architectural benchmark to refer to.

67 Westridge House
[Tudor House]
Wilf Crane Crescent and Banks Street, Yarralumla
1928 Harold Desbrowe-Annear
GC, V, NA

This unique Arts and Crafts styled residence was designed by the noted Melbourne Architect Harold Desbrowe-Annear as the Principal's Residence for the adjacent Australian Forestry School which was completed in 1927. Desbrowe-Annear is well known for his other style – essentially a stripped down, proto-modernist, flat-roofed and white-walled aesthetic – that he had some success with in Melbourne before the First World War.

With its pitched roof, half timbered upper storey and buttressed corners Westridge House belongs to his Arts and Crafts approach – similar to the early 1900s English work of Voysey and Baillie-Scott – which Desbrowe-Annear continued with well into the 1920s. Internally, the house features extensive, finely detailed timberwork, particularly in the major stair, and the living room has double-hung windows, which disappear into a spandrel cavity when open.

Charles Lane-Pool, its first resident, was Principal from 1927–44 and also Inspector-General of Forests in the territory. There were then only two other Principals before the Forestry School was transferred to the ANU in 1965. Acquired by the CSIRO when it took over the Forestry School precinct in 1975, the house next became home to the National Bushfire Research Unit. Recently it has been refurbished and conserved and the CSIRO uses it as an executive residence again.

In 1927–28, Lane-Pool had hoped to house the School's students in another new residential building. However, this was never commenced and, in 1928, the 27 students were housed in individual timber cubicles of the type used to house construction workers in the city at that time. The cubicles, each with an electric light, wardrobe, table and chair, no longer exist.

The Arts and Crafts movement began in Britain in the late 1880s as a reaction to the social and aesthetic decline, at all levels, caused by the Industrial Revolution. The precursor of the movement, William Morris, was vocal in his criticism of the thoughtless swing in architecture to Gothic impersonations and the factory production lines which replaced the craftsman's art.

Morris was a middle class worthy who set out to save the poor labourers from the squalor of an industrial Britain by establishing what he described as 'an earthly paradise'. The Arts and Crafts movement despised imitation materials and mock Gothic and Renaissance buildings. Instead it adhered to its belief in 'simplicity, truth to materials and the unity of handicraft and design'.

The principles of the movement had considerable impact in the English speaking world and contributed to the formation of Anglo-Modernism.

K18

68 Two Houses
6 Fuller Street [above] and 44 Beauchamp Street [below right], Deakin
1965 Dirk Bolt
GC, V, NA

These two houses, separated by only a couple of streets, are two different examples of Dirk Bolt's talent for residential architecture. Built in the same year, both have fair face concrete masonry, timber glazing walls, white painted fascias and flat roofs – essentially the Bolt residential vocabulary. But then there are differences.

No. 44 Beauchamp Street is a two-storied house facing north towards Black Mountain and it is built on the high side of a hilly road with the principal rooms facing north to this view. Its muscular masonry columns supporting simple flat roof fascias and the subtlety of some of its junctions are worth noting. This is an extroverted house.

Down at the bottom of the same hill, No. 6 Fuller Street is quite a different house. It is on a flat site with no view to speak of. Consequently it is more introverted and impenetrable. Entry to this one storey, flat roofed house is through a walled garden acting as a transitional space and screen from the street. Inside the main bedroom is at one end of the house near the entry and the other two bedrooms are placed at the other end. In between are the living spaces, which open directly onto a north facing terrace. Apart from the main bedroom, all other major rooms in the house have sliding walls that when closed, completely compartmentalise the house and when opened create a completely open area. All the original clear finished interior joinery and simple bathroom details are extant and provide a complete glimpse of the house as Bolt intended.

69 Bowden House
11 Northcote Street, Deakin
1955 Harry Seidler

GC, V, NA

Designed in 1950 but not built immediately, this two-bedroom and study, split level house is early period Seidler. It was his first architectural commission outside Sydney and it is the only detached house he has built in the capital.

As with most of his large corpus of work the Bowden House contains examples of specific design strategies or devices that Seidler used from project to project always in slightly different stages of development or in thematic variations that seem inexhaustible in their capacity to engender different, but consistent outcomes. Thus, in houses or office towers Seidler shows himself to be like a fuguist interpolating different themes over and over again.

One of his favourite planning paradigms – discrete living and sleeping zones – is arranged here in section to separate the two zones by half a floor level. The house also has its roof slope running parallel to the ground only to be kicked up over the living room terrace; another often used motif in this early period. At Northcote Street, Seidler also makes an emphatic point about the dissolution of solid forms into planes with the natural stone flanking wall that is inflected to accommodate the building entry in a most subtle way. The house has been added to twice – once by the architect – but still retains its slightly Breueresque, totally Seidler, character.

70 Benjamin House
10 Gawler Crescent, Deakin
1956 Alex Jelinek

GC, V, NA

This surprising house is the creation of a Czech architect who came to Australia in the early 1950s to work on the Snowy Mountains Scheme. The house, for a Professor Benjamin, is across the street from the only Canberra work by Brisbane architect James Birrell and around the corner from Harry Seidler's Bowden House [1955]. It won an Institute of Architects award in 1957 for House of the Year.

It is built from concrete blockwork with flat roofs and deep timber fascias, it is radial in plan and two stories high. The visitor is drawn in by a wall extending out to the street. Entry and circulation are at the centre of the house, which is divided up into radial segments and is split level in section. At the very centre of the house a cylindrical mast structure receives the loads from the roof beams, collects the roof water and distributes it to a pool.

The complicated structure and forms are well resolved and show a level of control that is usually beyond the reach of 30 year old architects. Melbourne based Jelinek also designed the Peregian Roadhouse near Noosa which was opened in 1962 and it is similarly startling.

71 Forrest Conservation Area
Melbourne Avenue, Empire Circuit, Arthur Circle, Hobart Avenue and National Circuit, Forrest
c1924–30 Various, especially Oakley and Parkes
GC, V, A

Developed as single residences and designed in the early to mid-1920s, to a street layout that was determined by a competition won by Oakley and Parkes, this core area of approximately 15 hectares in Forrest is a well preserved fragment of early Canberra as envisaged by the Federal Capital Advisory Committee. The FCAC, established in 1921 after the resignation of Walter Burley Griffin from government employment, and chaired by Sir John Sulman, was charged with the task of completing enough infrastructure and buildings to enable parliament to move from Melbourne to Canberra in 1927. Forrest was designated as an area for upper-echelon government employees.

The vision to be found here is developed from English Garden City suburban ideals. Essentially this translated into development that aimed to mediate between urban and the rural environments through the use of detached house types with capacious gardens served by generously landscaped streets and civic spaces. With its curving streets, range of interesting house types and mature landscaping the Forrest Conservation Area illustrates the approach very well.

72 Moir House
43 Melbourne Avenue, Forrest
1937 Malcolm Moir
GC, V, NA

This house that Malcolm Moir [1903–71] built for his family comes with an interesting anecdote. Angus Moir, the architect's son, tells the story of one afternoon in the late 1930s when the family and friends, on the front terrace spotted a tall, middle aged woman photographing the house from Melbourne Avenue. The mystery photographer turned out to be Marion Mahony Griffin, visiting Australia after Walter Burley Griffin's recent death in India. She declared that Moir's own house and the Civic Theatre in Manuka [also by Moir, but now demolished] were '…the ones that Walter would have liked.'

The Moir house has all its principal rooms facing north; there are four bedrooms, two living rooms, a formal dining room and a lounge built over four levels. Eventually Moir added the glazed north facing studio office with separate access as his own office, which is now the most prominent feature of the house.

The Moir family occupied the house, with interior fittings and furnishings designed by the architect, until his death in 1971. From then until the end of the century it has only had two owners and still retains much of its original character. There are a dozen or so Moir houses in Canberra, but this is the best.

M18

73 Town houses
3 Tasmania Circle and 2 Arthur Circle, Forrest
1960 Roy Grounds
[Grounds Romberg and Boyd]
GC, V, NA

This group of five identical two-storied townhouses with an attached single-story bed-sitter and a separate courtyard house share antecedents in Grounds' own house in Toorak [1953]. In both Melbourne and Canberra he used Le Corbusier's Maison Citrohan [1922] paradigm of a double height internal volume with a glass wall facing the sun and a one directional stair running up the side wall. In this classic residential design paradigm living spaces occupy the ground floor – including the double height space - with the more private bedrooms upstairs, but still spatially connected to the whole. Even though the 1953 Melbourne project was a detached dwelling, Grounds was perhaps the first Australian architect to use this radical medium density housing concept model. Less than a decade later he was able to test it more comprehensively in the Forrest townhouses. The houses have intact interior linings of limed timber with a gallery and built in desk and well detailed other joinery overlooking the living area.

   Prosaic construction materials are the other antecedent common to both the Melbourne and Canberra projects. In Forrest many of the houses are constructed from cheap materials including dun-coloured concrete masonry, timber window-walls and a low-pitched metal deck roof. The courtyard walls facing the street were originally rejected, but then allowed by the NCDC to complete the model setting for city living to which this project no doubt aspired and emphatically achieved. Sadly, there is little else of its ilk in Canberra.

The off street entries to the town houses

74 Clark House

[Dymphna and Manning Clark's House]
11 Tasmania Circle, Forrest
1953 Robin Boyd
GC, V, NA

Robin Boyd completed this house in 1953 before entering the Grounds Romberg and Boyd partnership. Academics Dymphna and Manning Clark made an early commitment to Canberra when he gained a teaching appointment at the University College that eventually became the Australian National University. This was their family home and it is here that Manning wrote much of his magisterial, six-volume *A History of Australia [1962–87]*.

The house consists of two parallel, light grey painted brick wings; one for the living areas and the other for sleeping. Internally the theme of simplicity is continued with light coloured painted brickwork and a predominance of natural timber surfaces. Above the glass link connecting these two parts, is Manning Clark's book-lined study, the sole two-storey part of the house. Compared with other things Boyd was doing at the same time, such as the Richardson 'Bridge' house [1954] and the all-steel Marriot House project of 1953, the Clark House is relatively conservative, albeit modern.

Despite his avant-gardism on the Melbourne projects, Boyd's mentality here seems more connected to his research into what could be called the 'Victorian Type' – a sort of archetypal, idealised house which attempted to embody both the traditional pragmatism of early Victorian building and pared back Modernism. Roy Grounds' 1930s and 40s houses worked with this theme which stressed the continuity of architectural ideas. The title of Boyd's 1947 text *Victorian Modern: 111 Years of Modern Architecture in the State of Victoria, Australia*, neatly captures the intention. At the Clark's house the simple box-like forms of the wings, the modesty of architectural detail and a gentle relationship with the landscape achieved through patios, pergolas and courtyard forms all celebrate this ideal.

Following the death of Dymphna Clark in the late 1990s, the house came under the governance of a family trust with the intention of dedicating its facilities to the support of scholarly and cultural pursuits.

For the latter part of the last century Manning Clark was Australia's most famous historian. He wrote numerous articles for newspapers, gave lectures, and addressed academic, cultural, literary and political organizations across Australia. Clark was, nevertheless, a controversial figure whose political statements were sometimes highly provocative. In particular his broad generalisations infuriated many of his more conservative colleagues. In 1981 he was proclaimed Australian of the Year.

N18

75 Forrest Fire Station and Residences
Canberra Avenue, Empire Circuit, Fitzroy Street and Manuka Circle
1939 Edwin Henderson and Cuthbert Whitley [Department of Interior Works Branch]
GC, V, NA

From 1939 to 1983 this full block development supported the main ACT Fire Station and, in the early days, housed the Fire Brigade and Ambulance Services staff. Presently the Fire Station is a museum and the residences have all been converted to other uses, particularly offices.

As Chief Architect of the Department, Henderson probably took responsibility for the design of this complex. However many of the design drawings were signed by Whitley, which suggests he had a significant involvement. The seven residences comprise two storey houses at each of the four corners with three two storey duplexes in between while the Fire Station housed engines together with duty staff. Built in panels of red and cream face brick with a regular pattern of windows and high parapets, the whole complex, but especially the residences, is a good example of between-the-wars International Style architecture.

The progressive tone of the design may support the assertion that Whitley took a leading hand in the design. Henderson's architectural style was generally more conservative, and as Chief Architect he would have had many demands on his time. However Henderson did go on a European study tour in 1936 and may have seen International Style works first hand. In any event he died in the middle of 1939 around the time these buildings were completed. With the exception of a major addition to the house on the corner of Canberra Avenue and Manuka Circle, the buildings are all substantially in their original form.

L18

76 National Association [RAIA HQ]
2a Mugga Way, Red Hill [open office hours]
1968 Ancher Mortlock Murray and Woolley
GC, V, A

With its usage of domestic scale forms, white painted brickwork, dark-tiled pitched roofs and a layout derived from the disciplined use of pavilions and courtyards, the RAIA [Royal Australian Institute of Architects] Headquarters captures something of the mid to late 20th century design approach known as the 'Sydney School'. Ancher Mortlock Murray and [particularly] Woolley were leading protagonists of this style, and although much of their notable Canberra work reflects an earlier period when Sydney Ancher was more actively designing, this project is largely the work of Bryce Mortlock even though the firm's elder partner produced an earlier scheme that was rejected.

As designed the building provided both office and residential functions, although over time the residence has been subsumed by office functions, luckily by merely occupying it, not by expunging it. Earth berms, or embankments track around two sides of the complex and allow acoustic and visual privacy whilst effectively planting the building in its setting at the same time. Inside, the white-painted brick aesthetic continues with brick tile floors and clear-finished timber joinery all unchanged. At the heart of the building the RAIA's Council Room must surely be one of the more poised meeting spaces in a city filled with such venues.

M19

77 Fenner House
8 Monaro Crescent, Red Hill
1954 Robin Boyd
GC, V, NA

Boyd designed this house before his nearby Manning Clark house, but it was finished slightly later. Other connections exist: both clients were ANU academics with Melbourne origins, hence Boyd as the choice for architect; both houses have similar 'bi-polar' plans comprising living and sleeping domains separated by the arrival and entry point; both have similar construction technologies and both face large glass areas north; and both homes are unique for a continuous occupancy by the original families over several decades.

In his field Professor Frank Fenner [b1914] is as famous as Manning Clark was in that of history. Working consistently through the whole of the second half of the 20th century Fenner gained renown as one of Australia's leading microbiologists from his work on the development of myxomatosis and on the poxvirus to help in the eradication of smallpox.

The Fenner House is set well back and diagonally on a large block that rises several metres at the corner of Torres Street and Monaro Crescent. The large setback has provided ample scope for the garden design of ANU colleague Lindsay Pryor who has created an appropriate setting for the architecture. Boyd's bi-polar plan works well here with the long dimension of the living room pavilion fully glazed and facing north, and the quieter bedroom pavilion offset to the south. Apart from a sympathetic 1982 addition to this bedroom zone, all of the original architectural features of the house are still viewable; brickwork is painted grey on the north-south walls and white on the east-west walls, the ceilings are lined on the rake and the timber framed window walls extend right up to the soffit line.

M19

78 Canberra Grammar School
Monaro Crescent and Golden Grove, Red Hill
1929–64 Burcham Clamp and Finch, Roy Simpson
GC, V, A

When Gough Whitlam, son of the Commonwealth Crown Solicitor, turned up for his first day at Canberra Grammar in 1929 he would have been confronted with a building site in the middle of a bare 15 acre paddock. The first red brick and sandstone school building, designed in an inter-war Gothic style, was the quadrangle east wing and cloister and it must have been under construction. In fact its completion enabled boarders to take up residence for Term III. Conviction that the medieval overtones of Gothic were appropriate to 20th century Australia remained with Burcham Clamp and Finch as they proceeded to complete the Headmaster's residence in 1934 and added further classrooms, dormitories, masters quarters, dining room and kitchen in 1935. Incidentally Whitlam prospered and eventually completed his high school studies as Dux of the school in 1934.

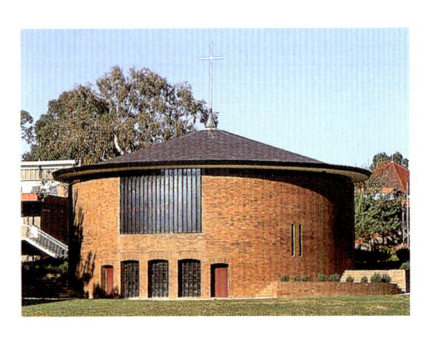

As more time passed, the campus expanded and Australian architects took up the cause of modern architecture in their commissions for Canberra Grammar. The answer to the question 'What style?' was answered by Roy Simpson of the Melbourne firm Yuncken Freeman who completed the enclosure of the quadrangle with an the almost-Miesian Science Wing [yes, it does have some red brick to match the other buildings] and his acclaimed cylindrical Chapel of 1964, offset to one side [below left].

The school campus is now even larger, but the interesting collision of mid and late century Australian values, embedded in the architecture, is still memorable.

79 Apostolic Nunciature
2 Vancouver Street, Red Hill
1976 Enrico Taglietti
GC, V, NA

Firstly, to decode the name: 'Apostolic' refers to the Pope – one who Christ sent forward to preach the gospel – and a nunciature is the office of a nuncio, the Pope's representative in another country. This large building set in suburban Red Hill thus marks the physical presence of the Roman Catholic Church in Australia. With its layering of floating roofs it is an arresting sight. Taglietti sees the Catholic Church as '…a large and dubious organization, with continuity – embracing, overbearing – over all' and perhaps this architecture captures that.

Viewed from Vancouver Street – with its emphatic horizontality and cumulative shallow pyramidal massing – the building is classic Taglietti, almost at his most pure. In fact it seems almost too big for the suburban site. The relentless horizontality is relieved with a cantilevered porte-cochère and a large cross emblazoned onto the building fabric. The chapel and its modified cupola are also noteworthy. Taglietti's non-residential work is aesthetically severe in comparison to the more intricate aesthetic of his early single houses. The bigger buildings like this one are both forcefully – almost ruthlessly – composed, but spatially fluid and meticulously crafted at the same time. It is this contrast that gives them a certain presence.

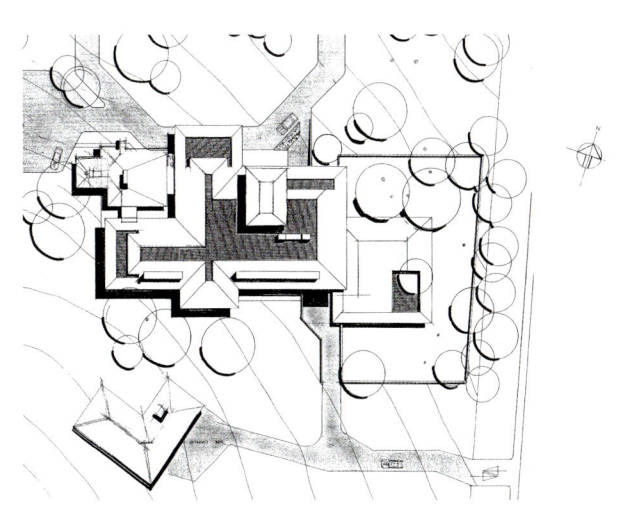

Site plan

80 Cater House
145 Mugga Way, Red Hill
1965 Russell Jack [Allen Jack and Cottier]
GC, V, NA

Talking about siting of this house high up on the block close to the road to get a view, and the consequent use of courtyards to maximise north orientation and screen walls to optimise privacy, Russell Jack, not long after its completion, called this house 'introverted in character'.

This accomplished four bedroom residence does have a wonderful panorama of Canberra to the north, but none of its principal living spaces opens up to the street – it presents to the street as a series of white painted masonry planes in a simple garden setting. It is a straightforward Sydney School work with the roof slope following the site, white walls, dark stained timber trim and a plan that supports an informal life style.

One curiosity though is the arrangement of timber posts across the north front. On verandas like the two living spaces, yes, but across the front of the bedrooms, where there is no veranda, just a small eaves, they somehow seem superfluous.

81 Baptist Church and Manse
11 Currie Crescent, Kingston
1929 FW Peplow
GC, V, A

Around 12 months after the Federal Capital Commission under Sir John Butters took over stewardship of the capital in 1925, it offered five-acre sites for the eventual construction of 'national' cathedrals and eventually six were allocated in various parts of the city. Amongst these were the site of the Australian Centre for Christianity and Spirituality in Barton and this site in Kingston, bordering Telopea Park on the Sydney Avenue axis, was given to the Baptist Church.

The Baptists were the first to move into construction and although Peplow's church was not the planned cathedral, when it opened in February 1929, it was Canberra's first major church building. The architecturally conservative pseudo-Gothic brick church and Georgian styled manse are contemporary with one another and are practically unchanged since completion. The church interior features well-crafted black timber and iron exposed roof trusses and a selection of fine timber joinery items.

82 St Christopher's RC Cathedral
Manuka Circuit and Furneaux Street, Manuka
1939 and 1973 Clement Glancy [and son]
GC, V, A

Depression era belt-tightening saw off the original project for a national, 4,000 person Roman Catholic Cathedral in Canberra on the so-called Cathedral Hill site above Parkes Way between Commonwealth Park and Commonwealth Avenue. At the same time St. Christopher's convent and school were completed and work started on the church after Cardinal Gilroy laid the foundation stone in the presence of two illustrious parishioners, Prime Minister Lyons and former PM Scullin. The church, built from specially moulded cream bricks, has been variously described as 'Romanesque' and 'Spanish Romanesque'. Clement Glancy's design is an early 20th century revivalist building in cream bricks that is derived from Romanesque architecture [the 9th to 12th century European revival of everday Roman brick building]. It is therefore a revival of a revival. The real point here is that it is not Classical and it is not Gothic, both styles that would perhaps have appeared too grand, too Italian or too English for the Irish Catholic majority of the day in Australia. By the beginning of the 21st century however, such subtleties are forgotten and most see it as just a rather big cream brick edifice of unknown ancestry. Nevertheless its rose window and clearly wrought brick detailing are still impressive.

This 440 seat St. Christopher's was opened in 1939, an occasion on which the then Prime Minister, Robert Menzies, gave an address. In 1948 it came to be called a Pro-Cathedral, and then in 1955 a Co-Cathedral along with the Cathedral in Goulburn. In the second major stage of work completed in 1973 the nave was expanded to 720 seats and the Chapel of the Blessed Sacrament and the campanile were added. Glancy's son, also called Clement, designed these additions and as the original brick moulds were still on hand, the building rather seamlessly doubled in size. By the end of the century St. Christopher's had become the seat of the Catholic Bishop of Canberra and an important focus for Roman Catholic life in the capital.

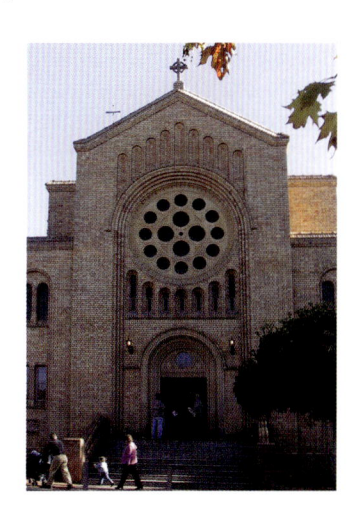

83 St Paul's Church of England
68 Canberra Avenue, Griffith
1939 and 1956 Burcham Clamp and Son
Stage 1 [four bays] dedicated in 1939, then completed in 1956.
GC, V, A

With its tower and Griffinesque overtones St Pauls is an imposing red brick presence on the corner of Canberra Avenue and Captain Cook Crescent in Griffith. It was the first Anglican Church built in the capital, although the parish of St John's, Reid, to which it belonged, was much older.

The church is designed in an interwar interpretation of Gothic which Sydney architect Burcham Clamp prepared in 1938 after a period in partnership with Walter Burley Griffin, so the Griffin influence is direct. Certainly the triangular shaped pilasters, the octagonal tower and the diamond patterned rose window tracery tend to support this connection. But the question of influence may not be that simple. Finely crafted brick buildings were more common everywhere in the inter war period, especially those by such well-known architects as Dudok [Hilversum School, 1927] and Peter Behrens [Hoechst Buildings, 1925] which received coverage in the architectural press. If we look at English practice, which may have been well known in Australia, even if the European examples were not, we find antecedents like Welch Cachemaille-Day and Lander's St Saviour at Eltham in London [1936] which has the same triangulated brick pilasters and a nave end elevation that is very similar to that of Burcham Clamp's St Paul's.

A mere four bays of the nave were completed in time for Bishop Burgmann's 1939 dedication ceremony, and it wasn't until 1956 that the remaining nave sections and the octagonal tower were added, also under the direction of the original architectural firm.

The suburb of Griffith is named after Samuel Griffith, the first Chief Justice of the High Court of Australia. Born in Wales, his family migrated to Australia in 1853 and the young Griffith went to various schools in Queensland and NSW country towns where his father was a Congregational Minister. He entered Sydney University when he was only 14 years old and graduated with first class honours four years later. Griffith then became an articled clerk in a legal office and, whilst still only 18, applied for the job of headmaster at Ipswich Grammar School. Having failed with this application he continued with the law and soon became a successful barrister, moved on into politics and eventually became Premier of Queensland. In the 1890s Griffith involved himself in the Federation movement and it was he who drafted the Constitution on the basis of a model by the Tasmanian, Andrew Inglis Clark. Obviously a lyricist, much of Griffith's spare time was spent on translating Dante's Divine Comedy *and a series of love poems.*

84 Houses

7, 9, 11 + 15 Evans Crescent, Griffith
1938–39 Malcolm Moir and Heather Sutherland
GC, V, NA

This group of four late 1930s houses was once six, but No. 17 and No. 13, also the work of Moir and Sutherland, have been altered – No. 13 irretrievably. What is left though, on this sloping curved street close to Manuka is an astonishing array of indigenous Canberra domestic architecture, which achieves a remarkable degree of freshness and architectural innovation. The combination of clearly expressed, cubic massing, delicate metal-framed windows – several in corner locations, flat roofs and well-crafted face brickwork is surprising and remarkable.

No. 15, close to the top of the hill, has a split level design with an entry separating the two storey bedroom section from a single storey living room pavilion. This house unfortunately has been altered with the addition of decks and pergolas at the rear and a coat of paint has obliterated the face brickwork. Interestingly, the Russian Embassy rented this house for staff accommodation until the late 1990s. Further round the curve and down the hill No. 11 is in pristine condition and externally is little altered from the late 1930s. Its play of the two-storey cube form, flat roof, metal pipe balustrading, window and door framing and sashes is exemplary and should be seen.

Even further down the hill, No. 9 presents a single storey pavilion towards the street which steps up to two stories further back. Its expression of chamfered corner brick chimney flues – two of them free standing, is striking. Unfortunately the architectural integrity of this house has been compromised by the addition of a faux Regency style front porch and bay window. Near the bottom of the hill No. 7, is a single storey, flat roofed house, which, from the outside, appears reasonably intact.

Taken together the four houses that remain from the original six offer a fascinating case study. Their integrity and cohesion developed through a consistent use of form, planning, materials and construction, coupled with particular individual expressions for each house give each of them subtly different characters.

85 Calthorpes' House
24 Mugga Way, Red Hill
1927 Kenneth Oliphant [Oakley and Parkes]
GC, V, A

This intact Early Canberra House is something of a time capsule. Harry Calthorpe was a prominent district Stock and Station agent at the time of Canberra's founding and continued successfully thereafter with real estate in the new city. The house is also connected to the Waterhouse family, through Doug Waterhouse, the early CSIRO entomologist whose research is linked to the introduction of the 'Aerogard' insect repellent. Just before the Great Depression Callthorpe chose the fashionable Melbourne architectural firm of Oakley and Parkes, who were undertaking other commissions in Canberra, such as The Lodge, at the time to design the family's home in Red Hill. The project was actually undertaken by Kenneth Oliphant [1896–1975] who had relocated to Canberra in 1926 to manage the firm's Blandfordia commission – the area now known as the Forrest conservation Area.

Calthorpes' House is still furnished and fitted out with a unique collection of domestic utensils and paraphernalia from the late 1920s that have survived without replacement as fashions have changed. In fact it is a one-family home. After Mrs Calthorpe's death in 1979 the ACT Government assumed responsibility for it and it is now publicly accessible.

With its brick and rough stuccoed walls, tiled roof, matching arcaded pavilions, it neatly represents the blend of English Cottage and Spanish Mission that was prevalent for the period. For better or worse the Federation craze passed Canberra by, so this style – now called the Early Canberra House – is given incunabula status in the city's residential architecture story.

86 Houses
60 Leichhardt Street [right] and 95–97 [above right] Canberra Avenue, Griffith
1939 Cuthbert Whitley
[Department of Interior, Works Branch]
BC, V, NA

Between them these three inter-war government houses and the two similar ones in Braddon, also designed by Departmental architect Whitley, constitute an up-to-date Modernist statement before the Second World War. Examples of houses like this are hard to find anywhere else in Australia at the same time, certainly in public housing.

Intended as standard government house types, the Whitley houses – particularly in street elevation – reveal the sort of asymmetrical abstract design first championed by progressive designers and architects like Mondrian, Rietveld and even Mies van der Rohe in northern Europe in the 1920s.

These small houses are moderate in size and tightly designed with economical forms. Exterior walls are generally of painted brick [probably painted cream originally] with raked out bed joints to emphasise horizontality They have low pitched roofs concealed behind parapets on three sides and an off-centre entry porch with a flat concrete roof and steel framed corner window – the windows are timber elsewhere.

The Inter-War Functionalist designs, which obviously influenced Whitley, had their origins with the De Stijl group amongst other things. This was named after the eponymous journal, which was their organ, espousing a total abandonment of naturalistic representation, replacing it with abstract art dominated by straight lines, primary colours and black, white and grey. The artist Piet Mondrian was probably their most famous member and Theo van Doesburg, Gerrit Rietveld, and JJP Oud the best known architects.

87 House
36 Furneaux Street, Griffith
1927 L Rudd and D Limburg
GC, V, NA

Canberra came a bit late for Arts and Crafts architecture to leave much of a mark. This British style which also took off in North America in a modified form, is well displayed on some fine houses in Sydney and other places, so this house is rare in the sense that there is little else of it around in the capital except for Westridge House in Yarralumla.

Turned to address the corner it sits on, Rudd and Limburg's two storey Arts and Crafts house with its steep roof shaped by hipped gables, chimneys and dormers, hung tile cladding, white painted joinery and low eaves it is a good example. It is roof dominated – Baillie-Scott would have declared, 'That house has a hat on it, as all houses should.'

Unlike the suburbs of most Australian cities, Canberra is free of unsightly power lines which restrict the planting of trees on nature strips. Whilst the power is conveyed underground along major avenues, the expense of continuing this in lesser suburban streets and crescents would have been excessive. Therefore the Federal Capital Commission ordained that power lines were to be run along the rear boundaries of residential blocks.

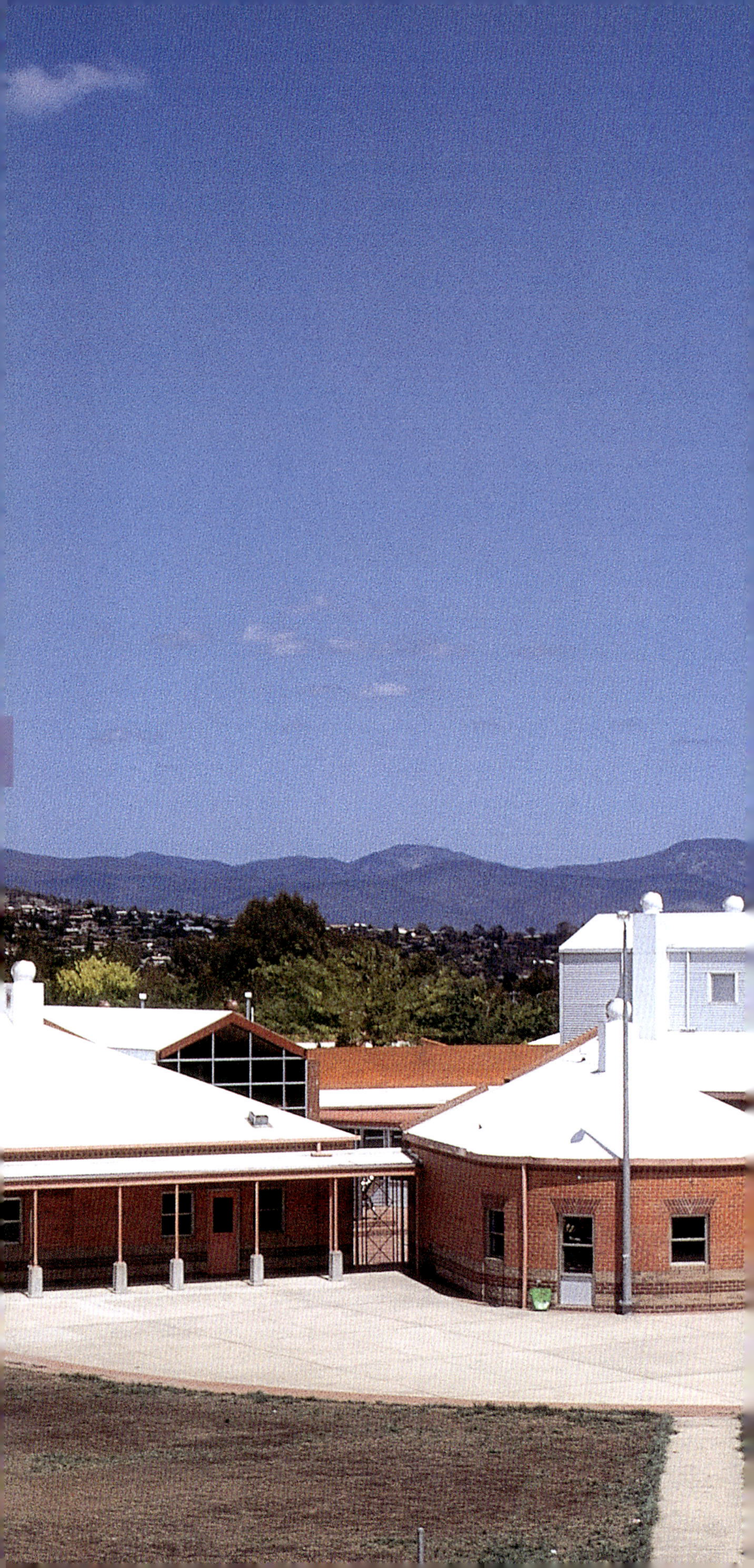

South Canberra

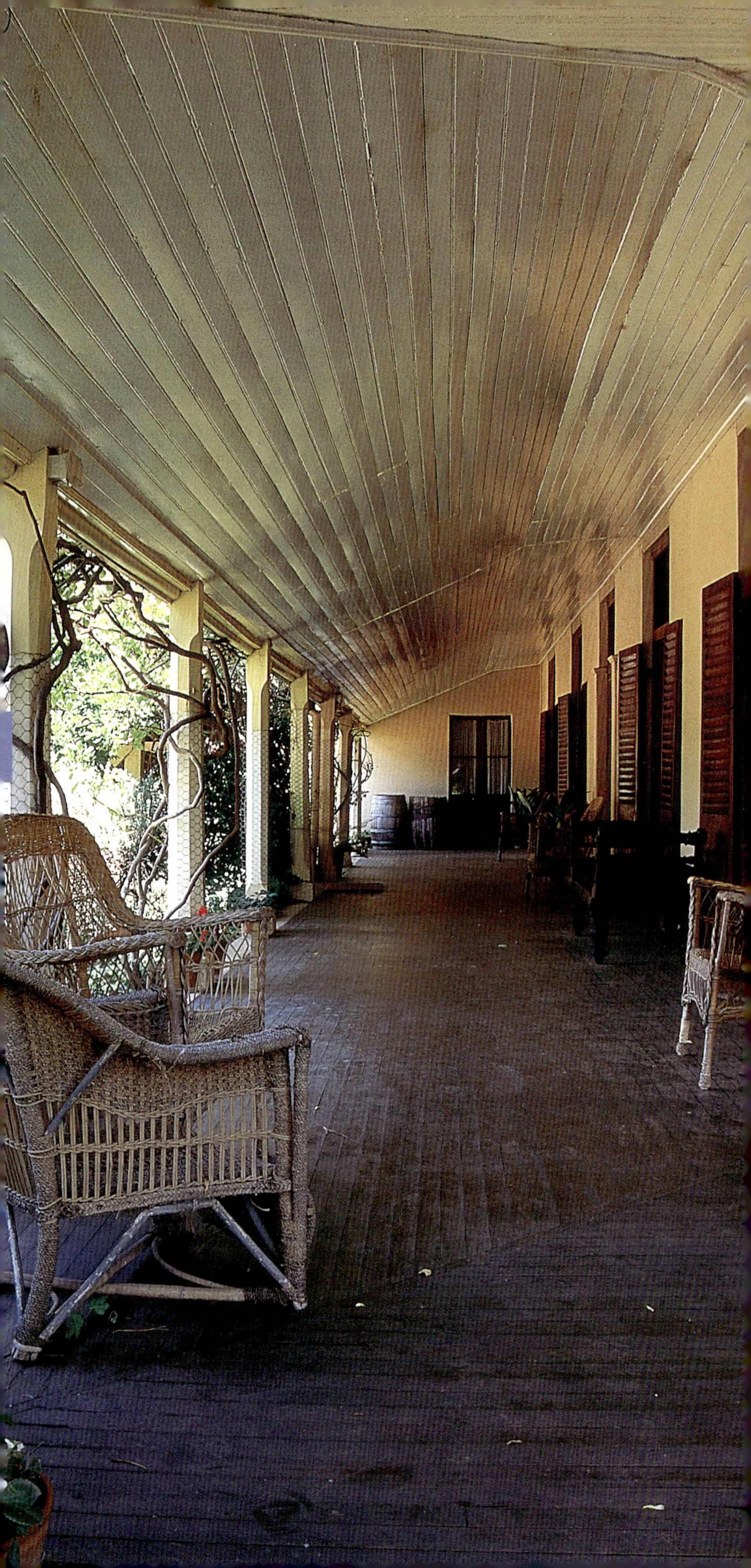

South Canberra

South Canberra covers a large area of suburbs extending from the southern slopes of Red Hill to the rural village of Tharwa with the Murrumdigee River bordering its southwestern edge and the town centres of Woden and Tuggeranong spaced evenly apart along the road corridor that traverses its whole length. These areas and the equivalent ones to the city's north result from Canberra's most rapid period of population growth in the roughly three decades of NCDC administration from 1960 to 1990. This was also the period when the Australian 'Baby Boom' population bulge moved into adult and parenthood. The Commission's planners quickly realized that growth would far exceed the 25,000 envisioned in 1912 and that the structure of a city designed for this size would not bear the weight of a 1200% increase in size.

Thus Woden, and later Tuggeranong in the South [and Belconnen in the north] were added to drag growth away from the centre and to ensure the policy worked, significant amounts of the Federal Government bureaucracy were sited in these town centres.

Whilst there are significant architectural works in South Canberra, they are not spread across all building types and are virtually absent in residential architecture. It was a period when the scale of residential construction became attractive to big builders and the mass housing that emerged is of no particular design merit, with a few notable exceptions that are included here. Schools, offices and public buildings of architectural merit are much more common in this part of Canberra.

South Canberra took the brunt of the January 2003 bushfires particularly in the suburbs of Duffy, Chapman, Rivett, Holder, Kambah and Weston where hundreds of houses were lost. The most high profile public site to suffer damage was the Mount Stromlo Observatory.

The front veranda of Lanyon homestead

B18

88 Mt Stromlo Observatory
Mt Stromlo Road, Mt Stromlo
1911–29 JS Murdoch, R Casboulte and H Rolland [Department of Works]
GC, V, A

Occupying a privileged mountain-top setting the Mt Stromlo Observatory was severely damaged in the January 2003 bushfires with the heritage listed administration building (pictured above) and five telescopes destroyed. A refurbishment project is proposed and funded.

The observatory owes its origins, according to legend, to a 1905 Oxford conference on solar astronomy where WG Duffield, an Australian attendee, realised an opportunity existed to fill a gap in the Western Pacific observation of the sun. By 1911 he and others had established the site and the first telescope was housed in a cruciform plan shaped building. This was JS Murdoch's first completed building for the Commonwealth in the ACT.

For the remainder of the century telescope structures were installed. The site expanded quickly to include administration and workshop buildings and residential accommodation including a Directors' residence and six other houses. Whilst all of the telescope structures are of interest, the most noticeable for architectural character appears to be the buildings completed in 1929 which include the residences and the Administration Building with its central hipped roof and two side pavilions, each one supporting an octagonal telescope dome structure – for the Sun and the Farnham telescopes. In its styling and mildly fanciful garden walls these buildings come closer than any other originating from the mid 1920s Department of Works to the Spanish Mission style that was emergent in Sydney at the time.

The site is also worth visiting for its other worldly overtones, meaning not just the world of outer space, but the mountain top close to – but out of sight from – Canberra. There are fine views over uninhabited mountain ranges and valleys that are memorable. It was here, as a resident astronomer's wife, that Rosalie Gascoigne began the habit of walking the hills and collecting the bits and pieces that found their way into her famous artworks.

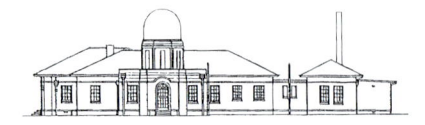

Telescope after the fire of January 2003, and above a measured drawing of north east elevation of the administration building by Hai Tran and Keak Tai

89 Orana School for Rudolf Steiner Education
Unwin Place, Weston
1997 and 2002 Greg Burgess, Paul Barnett
GC, V, NA

Orana is an interesting community based comprehensive school built on a 12 hectare site with an assortment of buildings catering for students from kindergarten onwards. Melbourne architect Greg Burgess and Canberra's Paul Barnett have both contributed significant small projects to the campus: Burgess completed the Kindergarten in 1997 and Barnett the Resources Building in 2001. Unfortunately the Kindergarten was destroyed in the January 2003 Canberra bushfires. Rebuilding is scheduled to occur before the end of 2005.

Steiner [1861–1925] founded Anthroposophy a philosophical system that focuses on our essential spiritual side and the effect of this on our thinking. In education this translates into students gaining access to their spiritual nature as part of their whole being, and in art and architecture this often translates into expressionism. It is interesting to see the effect of this approach on the Burgess and Barnett architectural works: they are sensitive, welcoming and warm. Playful even, but fortunately not coy.

90 Dingle [DeQuetteville] House
19 Downes Place, Hughes
1965 Enrico Taglietti
GC, V, NA

The interplay and contrast of horizontal planes of dark timber and serene white supporting walls underscores the external character of this quintessential early-period Taglietti house design. With scarcely a hint of a window in eye contact with the street, the architect's dual theme of sheltering privacy externally and spatial finery internally is manifest here as in other projects.

This deceptively small four bedroom house is built on a steep cross sloping block that opens up to the north with views over the Federal Golf Course. The intricate spatial sequence of the interior is arranged over three split levels that reflect the cross slope, and is just as intricate and rich as the exterior planar composition. Entry is organised though a small walled garden into a dining room and kitchen platform from here the upper level accommodates a full length living room and external terraces, and the lower level the bedrooms.

Over time the house has been well treated and continues to be occupied by owners sympathetic to the Taglietti residential design vision.

91 House
25 Colvin Street, Hughes
1960 Bowe and Burroughs
GC, V, NA

If this house is barely noticeable because of its unassuming, contemporary exterior, then its Japanese influenced wooden interior is remarkable. It is cleverly designed and thoughtfully detailed in well-made joinery using Australian timbers and makes full use of panelling and sliding timber screens to present a range of alternative functional and spatial arrangements. The house has only had one or two owner-occupiers and fortunately neither has seen any reason to alter this minor masterpiece.

A diminutive house perhaps and maybe the only one in Canberra by middle-ranged sixties and seventies firm Bowe and Burroughs, but this building is significant. The plan is simple and logically divided into living and sleeping zones spaced apart by entry and service [kitchen and bathroom] uses. There are others of this generic plan type in Canberra and it is one that Robin Boyd was fond of [see Manning Clark and Frank Fenner houses] and he called it bi-polar. At the arrival point and entry between the two major zones at Colvin Street Bowe and Burroughs designed a pool, which is not operative, but may be at some future point.

92 House
1 Astley Place, Garran
1967 Dirk Bolt
GC, V, NA

At the time of writing this house is 35 years old, but still looks fresh and wearing its age well even though it has been added to twice. The pronounced horizontal effect of the deep fascia and the frameless glass below set against hefty masonry columns are striking, but not loud.

The Astley Place site is well positioned to enjoy views of the Brindabella Mountains and the house responds to this with the large frameless glass living room wall set into the building's frontal plane. Generally the exterior, although constructed from modest concrete block and plywood cladding, is a fine outing in asymmetrical planar composition, a canonical part of modern architecture. Other innovative design ideas Bolt used are the application of tension cables to structurally support some of the larger spans and the provision of a natural ventilation system using shutters.

Dirk Bolt's revisited modernist residential work of the 1960s is one of the little known treasures of Canberra architecture. His houses in the capital are contemporaneous with similar work that eventually became classified as the 'New York Five', particularly that of Richard Meier and his very early flat roofed houses.

93 Australian Geological Survey Organisation Headquarters
Hindmarsh Drive and Jerrabomberra Avenue, Symonston
1997 Eggleston MacDonald
GC, V, NA

The AGSO complex is sited in open fields to the south east of Canberra and is most often perceived from the adjacent expressways in the context of a background of rolling hills. With their shallow curved roofs and large veranda and sun-screening elements, the two parallel connected buildings actually have a design agenda not unlike the school of contemporary Australian residential architecture centred on Glenn Murcutt. However the rationale offered by Eggleston MacDonald is based on energy consciousness as well. Inside, an atrium space penetrates the centre of all three levels in both buildings, and provides a logical means of internal identity and way-finding. There is also a collegial sense of purpose gained from allowing views into most of the departments along the atria.

This building is an appropriate Canberra example of supermodernity. This is not an architectural classification but one developed by the French anthropologist Marc Auge to describe excessively large and impersonal environments. In specific environments like airports and shopping malls, they have the capacity to overwhelm the individual and a sense of organic social life is difficult to detect.

94 Therapeutic Goods Administration Building
Narrabundah Lane, Symonston
1993 Australian Construction Services
GC, V, NA

This large Commonwealth Government agency building on a secluded site makes a cryptic duo act with the AGSO building just down the road. Both are rather bulky buildings on green field sites, however the TGA Building sits on more undulating terrain that makes for a much better contrast between the building and its natural setting. Roofscape is always going to be critical on a site like this so, advisedly, the building is designed with its roof as the fifth elevation and this succeeds. With its Y-shaped block plan and spines of expressed metal service flues it looks like some kind of hi-tech instrument. It also has three individually defined red tile pitched skillions running down each side to contrast vociferously with the green and aqua coloured exterior wall panelling.

All in all it is a good statement by Australian Construction Services – the Commonwealth Architects office – at the end of its life.

95 Canberra Hospital Diagnostic and Treatment Building
Yamba Drive and Kitchener Street, Garran
1993 Lawrence Nield
GC, V, A

There are notable contrasts between the original 700-bed Woden Valley Hospital [Stephenson and Turner, 1962] and Lawrence Nield's Diagnostic and Treatment Building. They look very different and that's not surprising given the passage of 30 years and the vast changes of architectural fashion and construction technology that entails – in 1962 brick construction in large buildings was economical, in 1992 it was simply unaffordable. Beyond these exigent factors however, Nield elected to stand the D and T Building in stark contrast to its older neighbour; he placed it at right angles, gave it a horizontal massing, used contrasting materials and colour and topped it off with a sculptural wave roof.

The D and T Building which houses ten operating theatres, diagnostic and administration centres, intensive care facilities and laboratories, is an impressive 137 metres long, 36 wide and 14 high. It actually is raised one floor off the ground so that its ground floor can line up with that of the older building.

After its completion Nield told a reviewer that it is horizontal because health systems work best when horizontal. The Nield signature wave roof crowning this monumental bulk prompted another critic to suggest the roof looked like a human body in silhouette laid out on a gurney.

From the west, specifically from Yamba Drive and generally in the direction of the Woden Town Centre, the D and T Building effectively dominates the hospital campus. In fact its effect has spread with subsequent buildings nearby mimicking the roof form.

Given the hermetic interiority of its functions this sort of building doesn't have much call for windows, they would probably be a distraction, so the exterior design is limited to the play of gum-green precast concrete walling against off-white metal cladding interspersed with a grid of smallish windows and biggish sun-shading. This is an unashamedly noisy building, which performs in the rules that it set for itself. It is conceivable to see it as the sort of colourful response to Canberra – the over-designed city – that arises from an assessment that the city is not urban or exciting enough and then wanting to do something to help out.

96 Callam Offices Woden TAFE College
Easty Street, Phillip
1980 John Andrews
GC, V, A

Intended originally as a TAFE college and meant to be larger than its present size, this complex of three connected office buildings – built partly over a watercourse – has evolved into office accommodation over its short life. Perhaps this is a testament to the adaptability of the design.

The project is an example of Andrews' additive mode [see also Toad Hall]. Here the repeated module is the octagonal floor plate fully glazed and supported on just four large columns. Structurally these form a central mast passing through the centre of each building module and emerging on the roof where they support four giant interlocking trusses from which the three floors of office accommodation are suspended. Glazing is sun-protected with an arrangement of stainless steel space framing and dark tinted plexi-glass panels, a system first used on the architect's King George Tower in Sydney, but now removed from it. All services such as toilets, air-conditioning and lifts are captured in free-standing cylinders around the periphery of the office modules, even the fire escape stairs are external to the office pods.

The powerful techno-expressionistic effect of all this is clear and memorable, but partly lost in the dizzying maze of bridges and escape routes that crowd the complex's entry court and lift tower.

97 Petit House
93 Brereton Street, Garran
1975 Ken Woolley
GC, NV, NA

Ken Woolley designed this large house for Sydney 'Merchant Builder' Brian Petit to take advantage of a magnificent north-facing block of sloping land overlooking the Federal Golf Course. Architect and builder had worked together before of course on the successful Petit and Sevitt range of project homes originating from Sydney in the 1960s.

Like some of Woolley's Sydney harbour-side houses of the same period, the Petit House follows the site slope with a multi-level plan, a mono-sloping roof and a use of unfinished materials such as face brick and stained timber inside and out. This house also steps and staggers diagonally across the site, creating walled courtyards, gardens and decks as it goes. The Petit house has a striking roof scape of skylights and chimneys, which should be seen from the golf course approach road [access from Red Hill] as well as from Brereton Street.

K22

98 Housing–medium density Swinger Hill 1 and 2
Barnett Close and Rowe Place, Phillip
1970 Ian McKay
GC, V, NA

In mid 1969 Sydney architect Ian Mckay who with Philip Cox had created Tocal College, one of the icons of the 'Sydney School', and who went on to design Paul Hogan's Italianate villa at Byron Bay, presented the NCDC with a design for their proposed 700 dwelling units on a hillside site in Phillip known as Swinger Hill. One of the most ambitious medium density housing project anywhere in the country for its time, the scheme included a mixture of semi detached, terraced and courtyard house types as well as apartments.

Only relatively small fragments – in Barnett Close and Rowe Place – were built to McKay's design with the remainder being taken up by private developers. With a 100% vehicle access mandatory for all dwellings, McKay had to find a way to get roads and vehicles into the extremely tight groupings of mostly single storey houses that were required to achieve the high overall site density. In the event he managed to do it with considerable variation in house type and form, but virtually none in materials, colours or construction techniques. This approach lends a consistency but gets a bit dry visually. Conceived as a tight network of densely packed private spaces, the housing lines the street spaces with little but high garden walls and carports, and has minimal public presence. Inside, there is a strong sense of indoor and outdoor privacy and the well thought out house plans function successfully.

F23

99 Housing–medium density
Pilbara Place, Fisher
1970 Cameron Chisholm and Nicol
GC, V, NA

Perth architects Cameron Chisholm and Nicol are best known in the capital for their Carillon on Lake Burley Griffin. This collection of modest houses in Fisher shows them to be adept in the very different milieu of medium density housing as well. Although the individual houses are competently [if conservatively] designed they do not stand out architecturally. However, to dismiss them for this would be to miss the point.

Instead, the objective here has been to create an ensemble that has an aesthetic consistency across a large number of houses but also to introduce sufficient variety to take the edge off the sameness that might occur in other circumstances. The Pilbara Place houses are not all intact, but enough remain to give a sense of the qualities the whole group must once have had. It is also an early example of Radburn site planning in Canberra.

100 Housing–medium density
Urambi Village Co-operative
Crozier Circuit, Kambah
1974 Michael Dysart
GC, V, NA

This group of 72 medium density housing units on the western edge of Kambah borders a golf course and is organised on a Co-operative Title basis. Clearly this assisted Michael Dysart to produce a uniquely varied residential environment which has strongly cohesive architectural qualities. There are 43 single storey units, many of them using L shaped plans with courtyards along the golf course side, and 29 tri-level units along the street side.

With parking consolidated into group garages the central space between these two informal rows is predominantly pedestrian and generously landscaped. A comfortable sequence of semi-private spaces conducts the visitor from public street to private dwelling with some grace in spite of the high density of residences and the obvious need for privacy. A restricted palette of materials and simple architectural forms further reinforces the significance of collectiveness and landscape in the overall scheme, particularly the central space, which is totally maintained by the Co-operative.

A similar project by Dysart in Wybalena Grove, Cook is actually larger, but less successful in perhaps not ageing as well as Urambi Village, but for students of medium density housing, it is well worth a visit.

101 Blue House
10 Decker Place, Fadden
1993 Rachel Bourne and Shane Blue
GC, V, NA

Nestling into an east facing, bowl-shaped Fadden hillside and backing onto the Canberra Nature Park [visible from the fire trail but there is a glimpse of the house from Decker Place] this project came early in the careers of Bourne and Blue. Built from joined pavilions of face brick and natural timber stepping down the hillside towards the road, this large house privileges the living room with extensive glass areas to take advantage of views, but operates with a more sheltered language of warm timber walls and smaller openings for the intensely private areas such as the bedrooms.

The prominent use of engineered timber and the aesthetic of expressed structure and junction that accompanies that, are well handled. Of particular interest is the quality of the detailed finish, since not only did the architects design the house, but actually built it too. After the completion of this project Bourne and Blue relocated to Newcastle in NSW and this is their only significant Canberra work to date.

102 Caroline Chisholm High School
Hambidge Crescent and Norris Street, Chisholm
1985 Lawrence Nield
GC, V, A

Apart from servicing the specific needs of High School education, Lawrence Nield had other objectives in the design of this picturesque Postmodern complex. Firstly, in order to look again at the institutional character of the modern high school, he cast the design as a miniature city or a village with a town square containing the library and a grid of 'streets' with 'houses', actually classroom blocks. Secondly, he hoped to create an urban place in Chisholm, a place representative of Canberra, the city sans conventional urban qualities.

Caroline Chisholm High School succeeds refreshingly in the first of these two objectives, but is somehow disappointing in the other. Perhaps Chisholm doesn't actually need urbanising, and is happily suburban. To say a high school can be a village is to use an appropriate architectural metaphor, but then to believe that a high school surrounded by open fields can carry a torch for conventional urbanism is probably over optimistic.

Nield's architecture succeeds in spite of his rhetorical stance. The regular grid of pavilions with just the library slightly askance, the distinctive roof scape using slope and expressed ventilators and the carefully detailed brick walls are all successful architectural ingredients.

103 Cuppacumbalong Homestead
Naas Road, Tharwa
1848, 1886 and 1923 John Reid
GC, V, A

Despite its 1987 conversion to an art gallery, Cuppacumbalong provides – especially, externally and in the garden – a significant glimpse of life in one of the region's largest rural stations in the first half of the twentieth century.

The Sydney architect John Reid designed the current house in the early 1920s. This, the third house on the site, used the bungalow form with a prominent veranda facing eastwards towards the Murrumbidgee River. Apart from the addition of a billiards room by a subsequent owner in 1932, the house remained unchanged for most of the rest of the century.

South Canberra

J36 cont...

Cuppacumbalong occupies a magnificent riverside site with formal gardens constructed in the 1920s. There is evidence in these gardens of two former houses: the original 1848 homestead of John and Mary Wright, discernible as footings in the ground, and the de Salis homestead of 1886. Both are located to one side of the current building in the vicinity of the tennis court that also dates from the 1920s.

The rhythmic name Cuppacumbalong means meeting of the waters, in the Ngunnawal language, and refers to the junction of the Murrumbidgee and Gudgenby Rivers near to the homestead. Close by is the single lane Tharwa Bridge, the oldest bridge in the Australian Capital Territory.

104 Lanyon Homestead
Lanyon Drive, Tharwa
1835 John James and William Wright,
1859 Andrew and Jane Cunningham
GC, V, A (closed Mondays)

Regarded by some as one of Australia's best homestead groups, Lanyon is a Murrumbidgee River pastoral property situated to the south of Canberra with a backdrop of the Brindabella Mountains. The Wright family from Derby built the first house. This same family also had connections with nearby Cuppacumbalong. This original stone house still exists and stands in the courtyard at the rear of the larger, single-storied main house built in 1880 of stone rubble finished in stucco. Other early stone buildings making up the courtyard include a dairy, blacksmith's shop, stores and a convict's barracks and small crofter's cottage.

Lanyon, a noteworthy example of vernacular architecture, has been restored and furnished by the ACT Government and has been open to the public since 1986.

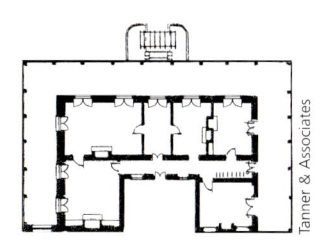

Floor plan of Lanyon homestead 1859

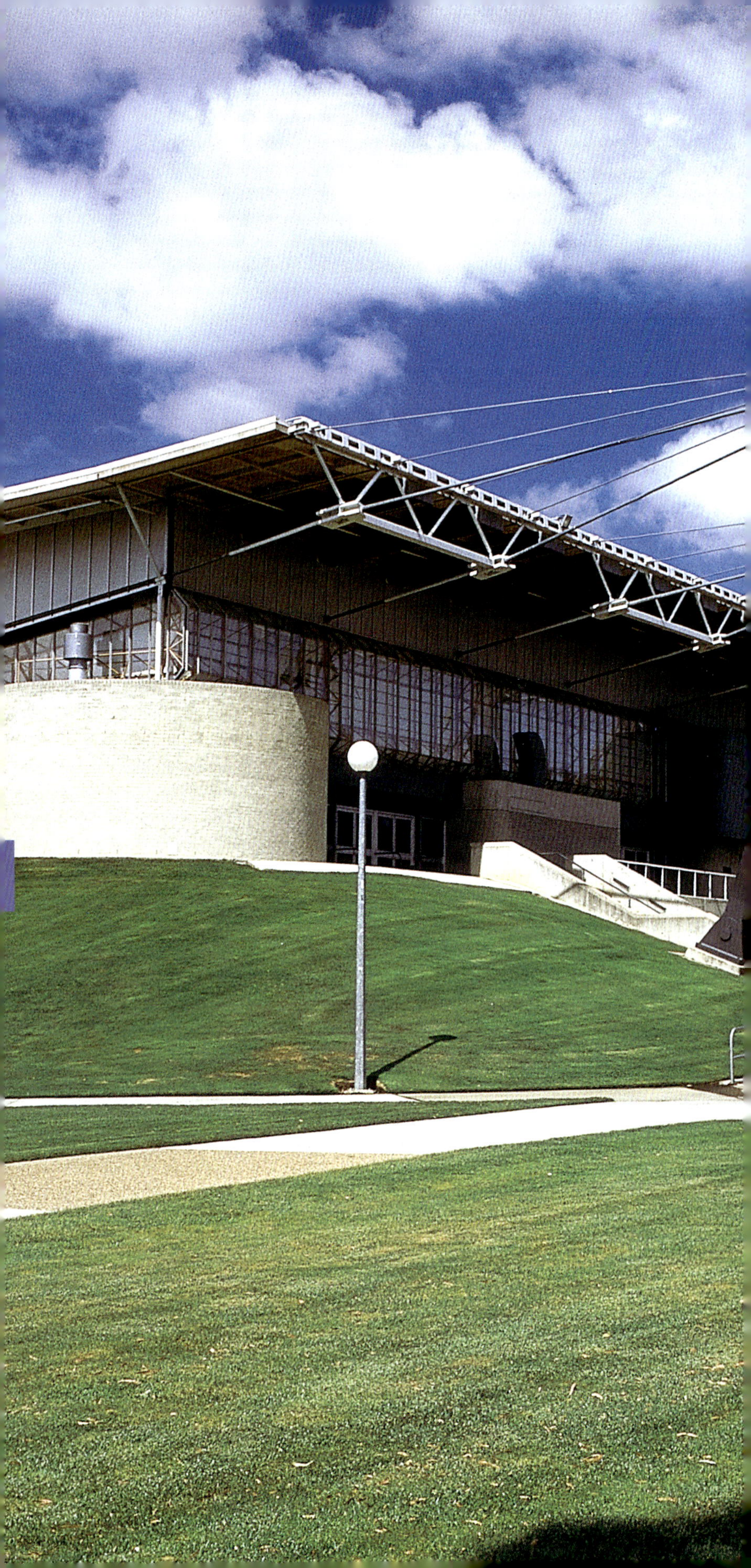

North Canberra

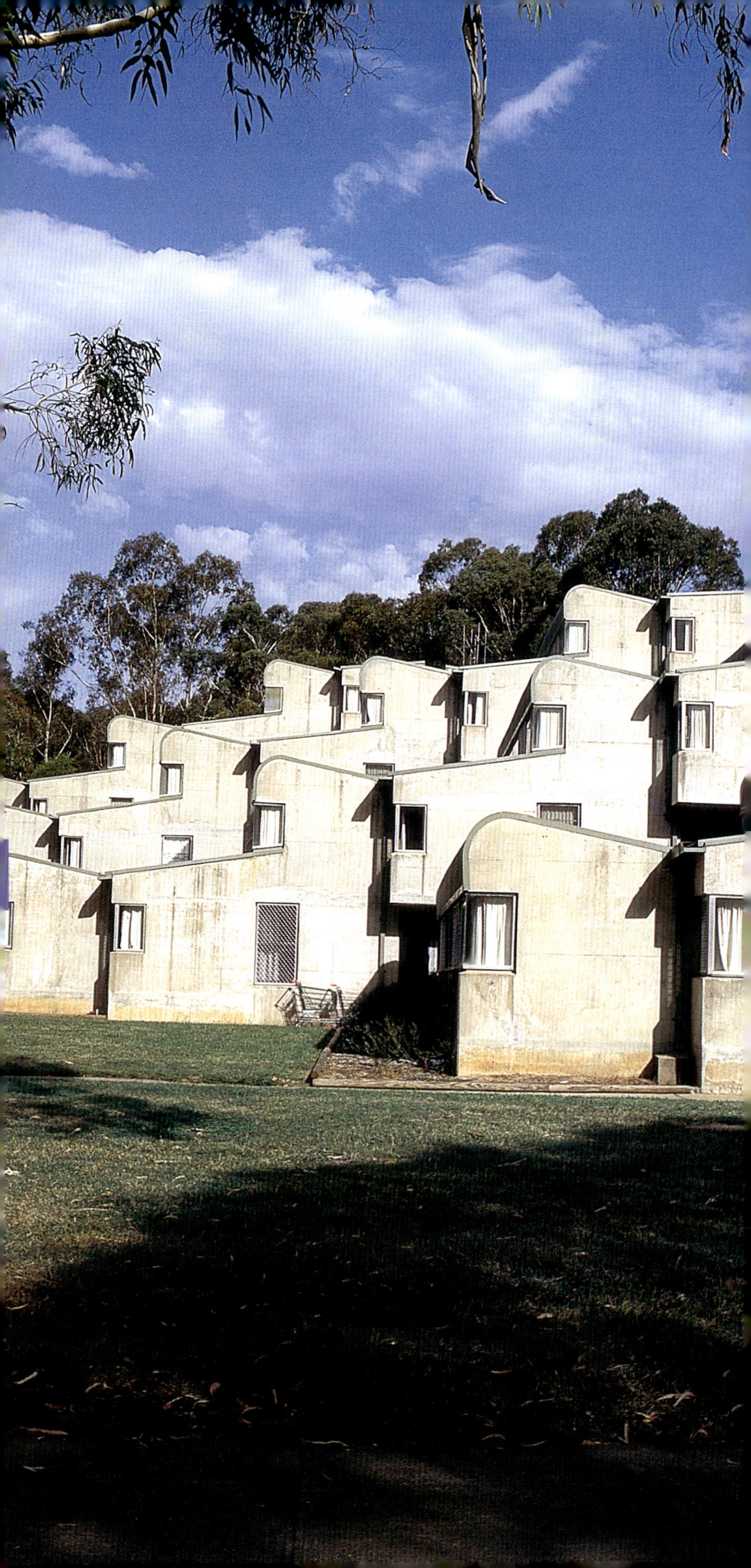

North Canberra

The national capital's northern suburbs were developed in the 70s and 80s over a vast area of former farmland separated from the rest of the city by Black Mountain, the Bruce/O'Connor ridge and the Gungahlin grasslands.

The Belconnen town centre at the southern end of Lake Ginninderra forms a retail, employment and recreational hub at its centre. Further to the north, Gungahlin took the bulk of Canberra's growth from the last years of the 20th century into the 21st. However, its centre, the first town centre constructed since ACT self-government in 1989, has no employment of the type which the Federal Government was able to endow earlier centres. Unfortunately in Gungahlin there is a dearth of architectural works of the quality found elsewhere in Canberra.

In North Canberra, as with the city's south, the scale, expediency and speed with which residential suburbs were constructed, meant that, with a few exceptions [Aranda for example], residential architecture of quality is also scarce and the involvement of architects has been slight. There is a different tale in the case of public buildings however as North Canberra has significant architectural works in the town centre of Belconnen, at the University of Canberra and the Australian Institute of Sport close by.

There are key works by Canberra's two *émigré* Italians, Romaldo Giurgola and Enrico Taglietti as well as prominent Australian architects Daryl Jackson, Philip Cox, John Andrews and Robin Gibson. For those prepared to move about on foot, the town centre, the university and the AIS are all manageable and offer rewards.

H12

105 Paterson House
7 Juad Place, Aranda
1968 Enrico Taglietti
GC, V, NA

The rather introspective, windowless and defensive street appearance of this house conceals a surprisingly different interior that is spatially complex. Taglietti says he compacted the house's footprint in order to disturb the bushland site as little as possible. Certainly, the visible external materials of mere grey cement brick and stained timber add just two materials to the field of vision, far fewer than is normally the case.

The characteristic Taglietti spatial thematic of complex interlocking volumes is brought into play here with each space connecting to the others and each room having views of adjoining bushland. This is an idea that may have some precedence in Adolf Loos' early 20th century Viennese experiments that he called *raumplan*. The Paterson House is perhaps the most private of Taglietti's houses but one of the more interesting.

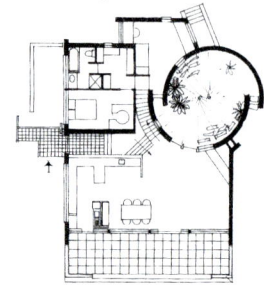

First floor plan,
7 Juad Place

106 Wilson House
38 Mirning Crescent, Aranda
1972 Roger Pegrum
GC, V, NA

In the 1960s and 1970s twin brothers Roger and Anthony Pegrum were scions of a burgeoning residential architecture scene in Canberra. Between them they built a solid corpus of work, mostly single houses in suburbs like Hawker, Garran, Campbell and here, in Aranda.

Roger Pegrum's Wilson house in Mirning Crescent exhibits a penchant for economical, natural materials and modernised vernacular forms that were current in Sydney at the same time. Fuelled by an interest in and manipulation of northern European exemplars, Utzon's 1950s residential work for example, this large house has a Z-shaped plan which effectively demarcates living and sleeping functions and orientates all rooms to the surrounding garden. Its mono-pitched roofs and large areas of face-brick walling proclaim a strong sense of privacy, if not orthodox domesticity.

Aranda was the first suburb to be built as part of Belconnen, the second satellite town (after Woden) in the Canberra area. The name Aranda refers to the Aboriginal people (and their language) who inhabited much of central Australia. The word Aranda may also mean 'throwing out little rays of light'.

107 Hyson Green Clinic
Mary Potter Circuit, Bruce
1997 Rodney Moss
[Munns Sly Scott-Bohana Moss]
G, V, NA

Hyson Green is a private psychiatric clinic operated by the Little Company of Mary Health Care of Calvary Hospital. There are 20 residential rooms in two wings together with a small group of high security rooms that orientate to the surrounding bushland. With residents sharing living and dining facilities, there is an emphasis on community interaction for therapeutic reasons. Other areas, such as an arts and crafts area and a walled garden, provide additional support to this idea. The roof of the central part of the complex is opened up with clerestory glazing which floods light into the nurse's station below creating an appropriate sense of place and occasion.

The architectural objectives have been to construct a sheltered, tranquil environment by merging the building with the surrounding native topography. The steel frame and infill tectonic strategy of the construction serves these objectives well.

108 Canberra Stadium
National Athletic Stadium
Leverrier Crescent, Bruce
1977 and 1998 Philip Cox
G, V, A

On the part of its government sponsor the National Athletic Stadium was an exploratory foray: it was the first purpose-built athletic stadium of any size in Australia, and the first component of the Australian Institute of Sport.

Philip Cox's design was remarkably assured in its handling of the site and the architectural technology of tension structures. Working with a low budget, Cox, who had no previous experience with this sort of large-scale architectural engineering, ingeniously spread the available resources by building the covered grandstand contiguous with an extensive earth berm, which encompasses the stadium perimeter and a warm-up track. In this way he established a monumental scale of operations for the whole project. To support the roof he added an imposing five-masted cable-stayed suspension structure, positioning the masts like a set of triumphal markers.

For Philip Cox the National Athletic stadium proclaimed an undoubted talent for a building type that, for the rest of the century, was to become an important output of his architectural office. The stadium, called Bruce Stadium for a while, became the Canberra Stadium in 1999 after it was considerably enlarged by the Cox firm.

109 AIS Arena National Indoor Sports Training Centre
Leverrier Crescent, Bruce
1981 Philip Cox
G, V, A

Like its companion piece, the adjacent Canberra Stadium, the AIS Arena is partly buried, so that from the exterior it gives little hint of the vast space inside. Originally intended for specialist gymnastics, with courts for tennis and volley-ball, the building seats 4,000 and has since hosted everything from High School Careers Days to Mahler's 2nd Symphony.

The stunning structural bravado of the whole roof being cable-suspended from just six pairs of giant steel masts set well outside the building envelope, is a most striking feature. After this the other architectural elements appear to following logically: clerestory glazing to accent the floating effect of the roof; a stepped cross-section that provides seating on the rake with smaller building functions housed underneath; and large brick cylinders at the corners to visually ground the whole thing. Cox's arena is an incisive architectural idea, boldly stated.

Remarkably, the Arena has been only mildly affected by the attachment of the AIS Visitor's Centre in the late 1990s, and is still an innovative, clearly thought through architectural work.

110 AIS Visitors Centre
Leverrier Crescent, Bruce
1997 Daryl Jackson, Alastair Swayn
G, V, A

The AIS Visitors Centre is a significant infill building that mediates between Philip Cox's AIS Arena and Daryl Jackson's own National Sports Swimming Centre. One of its main functions is to receive large crowds for events in the Arena, process them and move them inside – this involves a significant level change and as a result the Visitor Centre is dominated by a large stair rising almost from the door to the Arena entry.

The architectural concept has been to express the idea of linking and of rising up a level in the form of the building itself. Hence the whole building is canted up from the entry up to the AIS Arena at an angle of about 10 degrees. Its other main virtue is the large entry canopy at the northern end that receives visitors from the road in a most welcoming way and provides a generous covered space – something that is absent from most AIS buildings.

111 National Sports Swimming Centre Building 4
Leverrier Crescent, Bruce
1982 Daryl Jackson
G, V, A

Daryl Jackson's AIS Swimming Halls have come from a productive design idea of elevating industrial sheds to the level of architecture. The accommodation in this large spread out complex includes a 50-metre constant depth pool with retractable seating for 650 and a 25-metre warm-up pool. There are also saunas and spas, a weight training hall and accommodation for various coaching and administrative functions. Constructed in shed form with industrial-like steel framing and aqua-green painted fibre-cement cladding, this is a container building that makes a striking figure on the landscape.

Its facades are animated with primary trusses projecting through to meet steel external supports, by the expression of mechanical equipment and by a gradual ziggurat style stepping of the parapet line from the centre to the ends, each step indicating the line of a clerestory. Through a generous access policy the pools have become valued by the local community over the time since the centre opened in December 1982.

112 Bimbimbie VC's residence
Bimbimbie Street, University of Canberra
1996 Romaldo Giurgola [MGT]
G, V, NA

The Vice-Chancellor's residence is amongst the several planning, building and interior projects undertaken by MGT for the University of Canberra during the 1990s. Bimbimbie was designed during the tenure of Don Aitkin a Vice-Chancellor. His interest in architecture was motivated in part by the opportunity of working with Romaldo Giurgola who also redesigned the V-C's office and adjoining Council Room in the same period. However, the rarity of residential work in Giurgola's corpus also makes this project of particular note.

Bimbimbie is a large house but not a pretentious one. The program includes a private residence and, importantly, a separate reception room and dining space for university functions and activities that opens onto an extensive garden. The architecture is relatively straightforward and modest with a geometrically derived arrangement of white painted brick walls and pitched roofs rising to a peak above the Music Gallery, a small mezzanine over the 'public' entertaining spaces.

A salient stylistic point of this architecture is the chord it strikes with Kahn-inspired residential architecture in Philadelphia of the 1960s. This is a milieu in which Giurgola was active with other architectural luminaries such as Thomas Vreeland and Robert Venturi.

113 Student Residence Blocks I-N [Eggcrates]
Off Cooinda Street, University of Canberra
1975 John Andrews
A, V, NA

Nicknamed the 'Eggcrates' by generations of residential students and looking like a concrete Mediterranean hill village, these formalistically designed residential buildings spill down a north facing hillside on the western side of the UC campus. They have a dramatic presence when viewed obliquely from Aikman Drive.

John Andrews designed student residences in North America and two in Canberra: this one and 'Toad Hall' at the Australian National University. On each outing he deployed a basic building block of a group of five or six students in single rooms to make a workable social grouping with common kitchen, bathroom and living/dining spaces. The resulting architecture is then a function of how you arrange or stack these building blocks to make the aggregate building. Here they are stacked on top of one another and look like partially opened drawers. There are six such rows that vary from three or four levels at one end to six at the other. Access is via descending stairs which follow the slope.

Apart from the recent substitution of metal deck roofing for the original asbestos cement roof, the 150 room Student Residence is unaltered from the time of completion.

114 Information Sciences and Engineering Building
Building 11, Kirinari Street, University of Canberra
1992 Romaldo Giurgola [MGT]
G, V, NA

This large faculty building houses Computing Electronics, Engineering & Applied Physics, Mathematics, Statistics, Divisional offices and labs under one roof. Fortunately, the diversity of these uses is subsumed by the architecture, which has a powerful sense of combination not separation to it. This is generated through the disciplined control and severity of the building envelope, which is necessarily one of masonry and regular 'punched' window openings, appropriately recessed in recognition of a northern orientation. There is a straightforwardness and economy in the plan composed of two office wings and a tower of services at their meeting point which neatly envelopes all the building's activities.

In Building 11 Giurgola has responded to a somewhat overbearing University Master Plan with a conformity that questions its very rigidity. For example, he accepts the ubiquitous white brick but proceeds to temper it with a brown base course. Further, he rotates pieces of building off the omni-present orthogonal grid in a gesture that suggests a variety of other possibilities.

115 Lake Ginninderra College
Emu Bank, Belconnen
1987 Daryl Jackson
G, V, A

An orthodox paved quadrangle, ringed by a set of two-storey building blocks, is at the organisational core of this college nestled into the southern tip of lake Ginninderra. Apart from the Administration and Assembly Hall pavilions that are hinged apart to form the main college entry, each department – Science, Industrial Arts, Liberal Studies and Media Studies – is given a slightly different identity through the application of varying plan shapes.

The building structure is reinforced concrete framing, partly expressed on the ground floor along with white concrete and red face brickwork walls. On the other hand the first floor is generally expressed in a painted fibre cement panellised cladding system. The deep aqua colour of the latter appears as a further step in the colour experiments the architect first used five years earlier at the National Sports Swimming Centre.

With its diverse range of conceptual ideas, architectural forms, materials and technologies, Lake Ginninderra College is a good example of Daryl Jackson's inclusive and heterogeneous architecture of the 1980s. Later works in Canberra such as the Management Centre at the ANU or the CSIRO Discovery Centre seem more deliberate and controlled in their management of diversity.

Only hours after the above photograph was taken, Lake Ginninderra College was turned into a temporary hostel for evacuees from fire threatened neighbouring suburbs and residents whose houses had been burned down in the bushfires of January 2003.

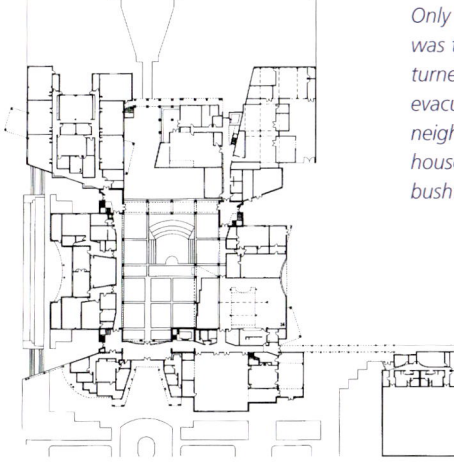

Ground floor plan of Lake Ginninderra College

116 Belconnen Library
Chandler Street, Belconnen
1983 Robin Gibson
G, V, A

Robin Gibson's library and adjacent plaza form part of a civic group located near a major bus interchange at the northern end of John Andrews' Cameron Offices. The library building is pragmatically and systematically organised to express a clear distinction between the spaces for people and community groups and the spaces for books. Accordingly the building's most notable feature is a spatial and architectural interplay with double height spaces and forms for entry, foyer and community functions and single height for the library itself. This doubling and halving – expansion and compression – of space is then expressed externally in extremely straightforward and cleanly detailed forms of glass framed by sandblasted beige concrete walls topped off with a massive concrete fascia.

With Gibson's adept handling of these forms and spaces the library still looks fresh enough. Its most unwieldy feature by far however is the rather low ceiling over the library stacks. 2.4 metres is the minimum allowable ceiling height in a residence, in a library area with plan dimensions of 20 x 20 metres, the space feels cramped.

117 ABS House
45 Benjamin Way [cnr Benjamin Way and Cameron Avenue], Belconnen
2001 Woods Bagot
G, V, NA

Although designed specifically as the headquarters of the Australian Bureau of Statistics this building, with its large central atrium space, is a distinctive paradigm for housing large organizations. An important consequence of the atrium is the realisation that architectural identity and social character emerge from interiority as much as from exteriority. The atrium design and interior organisation has provided the ABS with a means of generating a sense of common purpose and identity through providing an easily identifiable central space, common to all and accessible by all in the building. This space acts as a powerful visual focus for all users, allowing visual links between departments through a system of break-out spaces and sky-bridges.

External bulk has been lightened through the use of several devices, notably the division of the building into two wings with the atrium roof spanning the space between and a large blade wall defining the entry. A formal narrative of smooth materials and surfaces is interrupted with recessed areas to provide a sense of contained volume. The integration into the building fabric of graphic elements based on statistical systems, is a subtle reference to the nature of the ABS's activities.

North Canberra

118 Cameron Offices
Chandler and College Streets, Belconnen
1977 John Andrews
G, V, NA

In the early 1970s John Andrews returned to Australia from North America and a career that furnished architectural successes such as Scarborough College in Toronto and Gund Hall for the Graduate School of Design in Harvard. He had been commissioned by the NCDC to undertake the Cameron Offices project, the first stage of Belconnen Town Centre 10 kilometres west of the Civic.

Until recently occupied by its original tenant, the Australian Bureau of Statistics, Cameron Offices is a controversial alternative model for housing a large organization in a satellite city environment. The built design grew out of Andrews' interrogating the original brief for tall towers and suggesting an alternative, that they lie on their side like fingers with landscaped courtyards between them [see diagram right]. Andrews eventually built seven wings [or fingers] of office accommodation with landscaped courts and a lateral circulation spine bridging across one end of the fingers creating a point of address. The office wings were aligned towards the sun angles to allow shading of built space but still let sun into the courtyards. Executive offices for all the departments housed in the finger blocks were also located in the spine bridging all the wings at the street end.

Developed on a massive scale, to house 4,000 office staff, in Modernistic forms built from insitu concrete and glass, the Cameron Offices project commands attention. It looms large as a form in the Belconnen Town Centre that has grown up around it, and is an historic emblem of the 1970s city planning and architectural boom in Canberra. At the end of the 1990s the Cameron Offices passed from ownership by the Commonwealth and its future is uncertain.

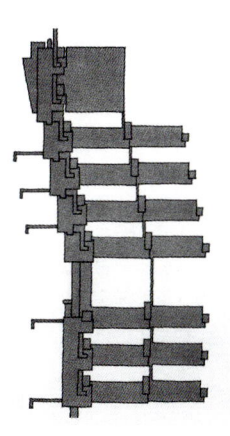

Diagrammatic layout of the project

G10

119 Housing–medium density [Emu Ridge]
Condell Street, Stapley and Dodgshun Courts, Belconnen
1978 Graeme Gunn
G, V, NA

Graeme Gunn calls these groupings of mainly two-storey and some single storey town houses, clusters. This particular cluster is typical of the 66 unit development his firm designed for the NCDC in that it is built around a cul-de-sac road which serves all units via their car parking. In fact, in this model of medium density, built for low-income users, public space is restricted to the road system and its ancillaries and all other outdoor space is private. Thus, although it doesn't resemble it, the site planning and the use of public space is identical to the ubiquitous 19th century terrace houses in inner-city Sydney and Melbourne. Instead of rows upon rows of houses Gunn, who was a significant presence in medium density housing in the 70s and 80s, has clusters.

With its expression of party walls, pitched roofs and balconies as well as high-walled private courtyards, the architectural manner of these houses is also similar to the terrace house antecedent. Here, however, the cast iron in balustrades and screens is replaced by timber and the slate roofs become grey concrete tiled versions.

The large Emu Ridge development occupies a site immediately south of Cameron Offices, it is linked to Belconnen Town Centre with a pedestrian way and it includes some five-storey apartments by Daryl Jackson. Looking back in 1983, Gunn conceded it was like a piece of inner-urban Sydney or Melbourne plonked into suburban Canberra, but he said it was an admirable concept for a truly urban environment, but slightly lacking in the urban interactive factor.

Graeme Gunn rose to prominence in Melbourne during the 70s with his innovative residential designs. In particular he made use of brick seconds, exposed stained timbers and open living areas which gave a whole new perspective to the project house market. For over 20 years he was associated with the landscape gardener Ellis Stones whose sympathetic use of native trees and plants blended perfectly with Gunn's architecture.

North Canberra

120

121

B8 **J6**

120 Housing–medium density
Drake Brockman Drive, Trickett Street and Mockridge Circuit, Higgins
1973 Enrico Taglietti
A, V, NA

In this group of self-effacing townhouses situated in Canberra's north western area, Taglietti found that some of his signature motifs were well suited to resolving issues such as privacy and car parking that normally beset medium density housing. For example there is a car parking building placed on the busiest street and the southwest orientation, which shields the houses and accommodates all of the cars so that the houses themselves are placed in a pedestrian only, park-like setting.

Then there are walls. Taglietti's use of walls is always to shelter and to discreetly reveal. In this scheme the houses are simple brick gable end terrace style houses with their party walls extended to form enclosing courtyard walls that protect the occupants from the public gaze. Walking though the public spaces between the houses, the regimen of public and private spaces is clearly presented, and yet the density is far from suburban. Talking about this project Taglietti recalled he worked to assemble courtyard walls that balance human interaction and dweller's privacy. He was trying, he said, to create an apparently effortless townscape of unique quality.

121 Giralang Primary School
Canopus Crescent, Giralang
1976 Enrico Taglietti
G, V, NA

Enrico Taglietti's work at Giralang Primary School was underpinned by a belief that primary education should not only be compulsory and free but also exciting and merry. The school is heavily sculpted inside and out, and with partitions, walls and openings carved out in an array of engaging shapes and forms, the interior is especially so. This is disciplined however by the framework of a six metre cubic grid and the concomitant geometrical rule that vertical or horizontal subdivision occurs within that module or multiples of it.

In order to reinforce the effect of what he called an adventure playground for educational use the architect arranged the floor plan to be open – with the partial walls and screens set out on the grid – and to step the floor up following a site slope. Externally, with its steeply pitched roofs, buttressed brick gable ends, deep horizontal fascias, and playful embellishments, the school is vintage Taglietti even though he suggested, when he wrote about it a few years later, that the external shape of the school was not pre-designed but became a controlled architectural result of the internal spaces transmitted to the exterior.

122 Norwood Park Crematorium
Sandford Street, Mitchell
1968 Roseman, Hastings and Soret
G, V, A

Norwood Park is the only Canberra project by this little known Melbourne firm with Peter Soret as partner in charge. With the skilled use of floating planes of flat roof, extended blade walls, and courts with reflecting pools there is a reassuring lightness of touch in this building that reflects the combination of dignity and other-worldliness expected in a crematorium. This, after all, is a place where the elegy of life is sung and the technological means of disposal exist considerately side-by-side, but never seeming to touch.

In particular the horizontal line of the fascia covering the entry porch, lobby and chapel atop frameless glass over the opposing pair of extended blade walls either side of the entry doors makes a nice composition. Inside, the presence of the exterior looms large through vision into the two lateral courtyards with their narrow reflecting pools. If required these courtyards and the lobby can be used for large congregations.

123 Australian War Memorial Annex
4 Callan Street, Mitchell
1978 Enrico Taglietti
G, V, NA

This large Taglietti work is one of his more proficient. Built to take the pressure of space off the main War Memorial complex in Campbell, the Annex houses War Memorial items and the conservation processes accompanying them. Designing to occupy a complete block in nondescript Mitchell, Taglietti created an urban interface by constructing a virtually continuous three metre high off-form concrete perimeter wall. This is literally urban rather than symbolically so in that the block is well defined and there is no purposeless space left over at the street edge. In fact, along the busiest street, the building cantilevers out over the boundary to provide shelter for pedestrians. However the perimeter wall doesn't conceal the buildings inside but screens them – in fact there are carefully located openings and gaps in the wall as well. The idea of screening with walls in this way is a familiar Taglietti device, it appears in most of his houses too; it's almost as if he sees that one of the functions of architecture is to enfold and enwrap the occupants of a building.

Inside the large compound a complex of brick – in contrast to the off-form concrete – pavilions, houses the Annex functions with its highest part bisecting the compound and actually bursting out through the perimeter wall at both ends. The architectural play of these wall and roof elements with the trademark Taglietti deep, timber horizontal fascias as well as the sharp verticality of brick flues, makes a most agreeable architectural ensemble which has just the right balance between a sense of order and the episodic departures from it.

D5

124 St Thomas Aquinas Church
Lhotsky Street, Charnwood
1990 Romaldo Giurgola
[Mitchell Giurgola Thorp]

G, V, A

This charismatic local Catholic church in Charnwood was one of the first projects Romaldo Giurgola undertook after the completion of Parliament House. In fact its genesis dates from an approach made by an energetic parish priest, probably around the time of Parliament's completion in 1988.

Instead of isolating the rather prosaic existing building Giurgola engaged it with an entry court serving both it and the new church. A courtyard, replete with Stations of the Cross makes up the third element reached from this new entry space. The use of courtyard walls to bind these elements together is conspicuous, but effective.

The church itself is a simple, steep skillion roof rising to an apex over the altar. Internally the roof is timber lined in contrast to the white plaster and deep blue carpet floor. At the same time as maintaining this strong overall form Giurgola has manipulated the lower sections of the side walls to create long recesses awash with natural light which are a reinterpretation of traditional side aisles. Elsewhere he has designed the central third of the altar end wall to create a full height projection that is adorned with a simple cross form cut into the external brickwork – this is also glazed to permit the entry of light in the form of the cross. The project is also noteworthy for the inclusion of a series of art and craftworks co-ordinated by Pam Berg, one of the architect's partners.

Glossary

Acanthus a herbaceous plant whose leaves were used as a decorative motif in classical architecture.

Architrave ornamental moulding around exterior of arch, doorway, or window.

Arris the sharp edge formed by angular contact of two planes.

Atrium an interior space of a building either open to the sky or covered with a skylight.

Baluster a slender upright post supporting a rail. Usually in sequence, thus balustrade.

Barge board a board running along the edge of the gable of a house.

Battlement an indented parapet.

Bond a method of placing bricks or stone so that the whole is bound together in one mass.

Bossaged stones [usually in columns] left uncut and projecting, often to be carved later.

Buttress a structure of brick, stone or wood built against a wall to support or strengthen it.

Cantilever a structural projection supported from a wall or column, such as a beam or balcony, which is unsupported at its outermost edge.

Capital the uppermost part of a column, usually decorated.

Casement a frame which forms a window that opens outwards on hinges.

Castellated built like a castle with battlements.

Clerestory the highest level of the nave or transept of a church containing windows clear of adjacent roofs.

Console an ornamented bracket or corbel which projects about half its height.

Coping the top course of a brick or stone wall, usually sloping, which throws off the rain.

Corbel a timber or stone projection from a building which supports a load.

Cornice a horizontal projection crowning the top of a building; also the moulding around the wall where it joins the ceiling.

Cupola a small dome-shaped structure forming the roof of a building. The word is used to describe the ceiling of a dome.

Curtain wall the non load-bearing skin, usually of glass, that encloses the framework of a building.

Dado the finished lower part of the wall of a room.

Dentil a type of moulding consisting of small (toothlike) rectangular blocks.

Dormer a projecting vertical window in a sloping roof.

Glossary

Eaves the lower edges of a roof, that overhang the walls.

Entablature the horizontal assemblage, in classical architecture, above the column. It comprises architrave, frieze and cornice.

Entasis almost imperceptible swelling of the shaft of a column.

Fanlight the window above a door usually, but not always, in the shape of a fan.

Fascia a flat horizontal band or moulding of stone or wood.

Finial an ornamental piece on top of a gable, spire or other roof projection.

Formwork a temporary construction of wood or metal either into or on top of which concrete is poured.

Frieze a decorative band at the top of an interior wall. In classical architecture it is the middle division of the entablature.

Gable the vertical triangular part of an external wall at the end of a ridged roof.

Galvanize to coat one metal with another by means of an electro–chemical action. Most coatings are of zinc.

Header a brick or stone laid with its end or head in the face of the wall.

Hip a projecting inclined edge on a roof extending from the ridge or apex to the eaves.

Joist one of the timbers on to which a floor or ceiling is attached.

Keystone the wedge-shaped central stone which locks an arch in place.

Lantern a small superstructure on a dome or roof to provide lightor ventilation.

Lintel a horizontal member of timber, concrete, stone or metal, which supports the weight above a door or window opening.

Loggia an arcade or gallery with one or more of its sides open to the air.

Louvre an arrangement of overlapping slats of glass, timber, or other thin material in such a way to allow flow of air but exclude rain, or light if opaque.

Mansard a roof with a double pitch, the lower section being longer and steeper than the upper.

Moulding an ornamental contoured band either carved or in relief used to add interest to a wall or surface.

Mullion a vertical member that divides the surfaces of a window, door or panel, often used decoratively as well as to add support to a frame.

Niche a shallow hollow in a wall intended to contain a statue or ornamental object.

Nogging a non-structural horizontal piece of framing used to provide support to brickwork or internal plastering.

Order the design, arrangement and proportion of all parts of a column and its entablature allowing for a method of classification. The Classical Orders include Greek (Doric, Ionic, Corinthian) and Roman (Tuscan, Doric, Ionic, Corinthian, Composite) examples.

Oriel a projecting bay window often of polygonal plan supported at an upper level by brackets or corbels.

Parapet the part of a wall that continues past the eaves line of a roof to give protection and conceal roofing surfaces and drainage.

Pediment a triangular low gable found in many classical buildings and similarly used in varying geometrical forms to decorate a window, doorway, archway or other wall opening.

Pergola a system of posts supporting a lattice roof intended for climbing plants and vines.

Peristyle a row of columns surrounding a building or open court.

Pilaster a flattened, shallow column that protrudes slightly from a wall, acting as a decorative element rather than being structure.

Portico a colonnade or roofed entrance open on at least one side.

Prestressed a condition of concrete where high-strength steel cables are used as reinforcement instead of steel rods. The cables are placed in ducts cast in the concrete and then stressed, inducing compression in the concrete before it is loaded.

Purlin a horizontal roof beam placed parallel with the upper wall plate and the ridge beam at regular intervals along the slope of the roof, in order to support rafters.

Quoins decorative or reinforcing corner stones of a building.

Rafter one of the construction members of a roof giving slope and form, as well as support to the external surface material.

Reinforced concrete concrete strengthened by steel bars or steel mesh placed in formwork before concrete is poured.

Reveal the side of a window or door opening showing the thickness of the wall.

Riser the vertical part of a step connecting two treads in a stair.

Roundel a circular decorative panel, window or plaque.

Rusticate stonework finished with a rough surface and deeply cut bevelled joints . Various types include diamond-pointed, cyclopaean and vermiculated (worm-eaten).

Sash a frame which holds the glass of a window. A sash window is created using two or more vertically sliding sashes, usually counter-weighted.

Skillion a one-way single pitched roof falling from the highest point of a structure to the lowest at the opposite side.

Space-frame a triangulated framework which encloses a space. The members of the framework are interconnected and are frequently used to cover large spaces without need for intermediate supports.

Spandrel the roughly triangular space between adjoining arches or above the curve of a single arch, bound by the rectangular frame enclosing it.

Stile the vertical framing member in joinery, used most frequently in doors and windows.

String course a projecting course, moulding or band running horizontally across a facade.

Stud a vertical supporting member of a timber wall frame on to which wall coverings and linings are fixed.

Stylobate a continuous stepped base supporting a colonnade.

Tensioning the process of applying a permanent stress opposite to that expected from the working load, used in structural reinforced concrete work.

Terracotta a fired clay material of red-brown colouring that can be molded or shaped .

Transom the horizontal member that divides the surfaces of a window, door or panel.

Tread the flat horizontal part of a step connecting two risers in a stair.

Truss a structural framework of timber or iron with increasing load bearing capacities used in the construction of bridges and roofing systems.

Tuck pointing the process of applying a narrow strip of mortar over the face of the joints in brickwork to giving the appearance of precision and regularity.

Valance a decorative strip or border edging below a roof, usually running between veranda posts.

Vault an arched structure of stone or brick, sometimes imitated in stucco, plaster or timber, usually serving as a roof or ceiling.

Voussoirs wedge-shaped stone blocks or bricks, which combine to form an arch or vault.

Wattle and daub a system of wall construction involving the interlacing of slim pieces of wood (wattles) which are then fixed to framing members and thickly plastered with mud (daub).

Weatherboard one of a series of long thin boards fixed horizontally with overlapping edges, acting as an external wall covering.

PHILIP GOAD

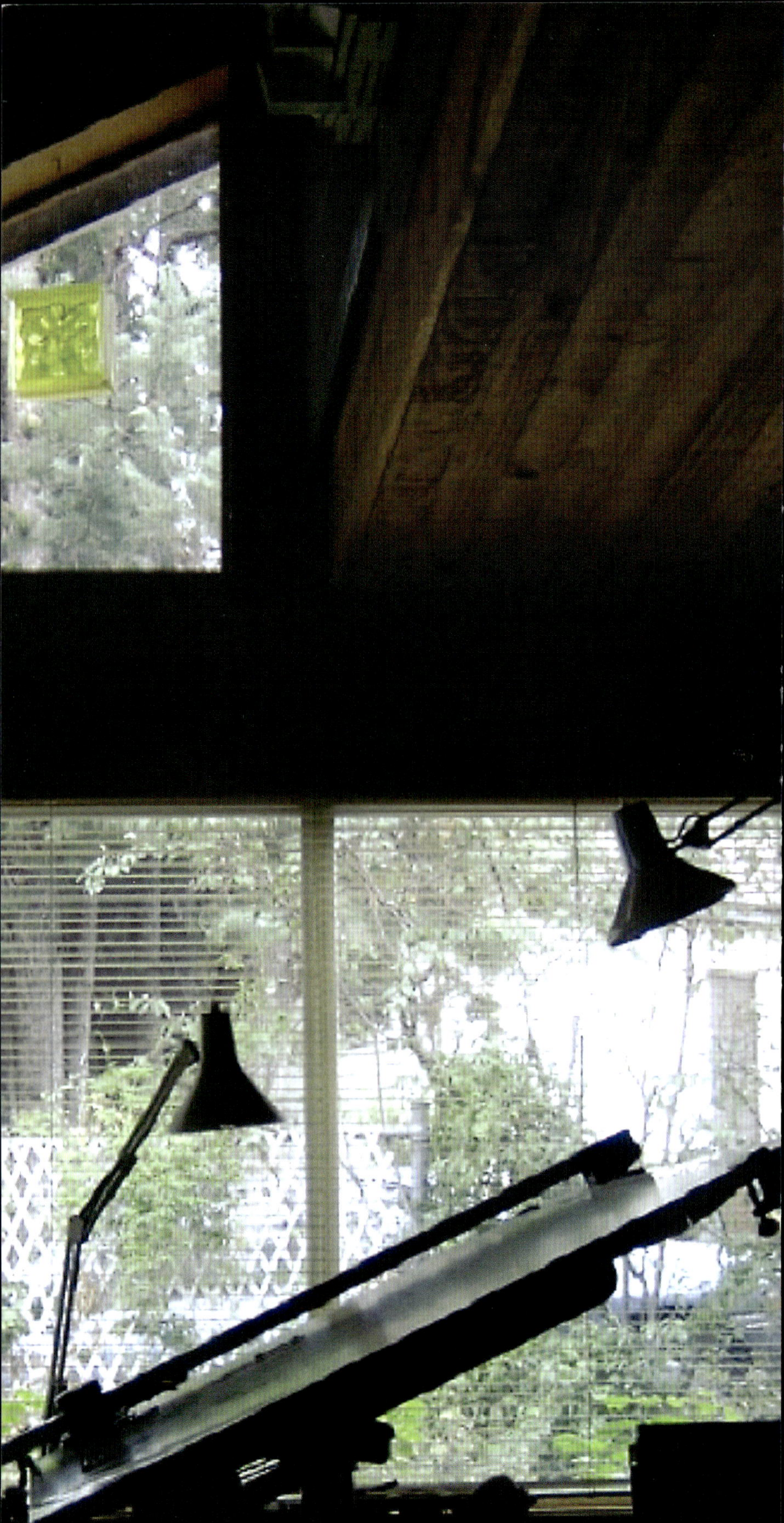

Canberra Architects

*I*f 'Canberra Architect' means someone who lives in the place and produces architectural work at a national standard for a number of years in the same way as one might talk of a Sydney or a Melbourne Architect then Canberra Architects are rare indeed. This is especially so in the period 1911–90, the years of Federal Government administration. Of the many architects included in this book perhaps only Malcolm Moir, Enrico Taglietti and Roger Pegrum conform to that mould. However Moir and Taglietti came to Canberra as adults with architectural qualifications and although Pegrum grew up in Canberra, he left to study architecture and left again in mid-career to teach at Sydney University.

Then there are others who have lived and worked in Canberra for only part of their careers. Cuthbert Whitley and Romaldo Giurgola for example.

And although they are famous for their contribution to Canberra, Walter Burley Griffin and Marion Mahony Griffin never lived in the city they dreamed up. Their entire Australian sojourn was split between Melbourne and Sydney.

The fact is most Canberra architecture has been produced by outsiders and this situation probably didn't change until around the end of the 20th century. Architectural work in the years of Federal administration was procured firstly from architectural staff within the various iterations of the Commonwealth agency concerned with the design and construction of Commonwealth building projects. Hence JS Murdoch and Cuthbert Whitley both worked for such an office in the Department of the Interior and Malcolm Moir worked for the Federal Capital Commission.

The largest contributors to Canberra architecture have been the prominent architects engaged by the National Capital Development Commission during the city's rapid growth stage from 1960 to 1990. In this group well known names like Seidler, Andrews, Madigan, Cox, Jackson, Denton Corker Marshall, Nield, Simpson, Woolley, Edmund and Corrigan, Gibson and Simpson appear. In this period, so the rhetoric went, if you weren't working in Canberra something was amiss. Grounds Romberg and Boyd, sandwiched between the Government team and the NCDC 'all-stars' don't seem to fit the usual categories. In the 1950s and 60s they did a lot of work in the capital, but none, or very little, for public clients – unless you can count the Australian National University as a public client. Finally, since the dissolution of Federal administration, local architectural firms have flourished, so that now local architects like Rodney Moss, Graham Humphries, Colin Stewart, Ric Butt, Phil Page and Alastair Swayn, some working in association with interstate firms, are predominant.

Walter Burley Griffin [1876–1937]
Marion Mahony Griffin [1871–1961]

Compared to his early mentor Frank Lloyd Wright, Walter Burley Griffin had a relatively short career and yet he was professionally active in the United States, Australia and India. Along with Louis Sullivan and Wright, both Griffins were at the centre of the Prairie School, America's first original architectural style.

Walter Burley Griffin was born in Maywood Illinois in 1876, spent his high school years in Chicago and studied architecture at the University of Illinois under Nathan Ricker who stressed the technical nature of architecture in preference to the merely artistic. He graduated in 1899 and worked initially at Steinway Hall, an early Chicago high-rise building, that had a coterie of progressive architects [called 'the 18'] sharing space and facilities together. By 1901 he'd become a registered architect in the state of Illinois, started working for Wright at his Oak Park studio and had accepted his first private commissions. After a falling out with Wright in 1906, Griffin established his own practice in Chicago and by 1914 had created around 125 projects, roughly half of which were built. Those still standing include houses in Illinois for Emery [1903], R Griffin [1909], Sloane and Carter [1910], Blount [1911], the Cooley House, Louisiana [1909] and the Stinson Library, Illinois [1914]. The best intact group of Griffin houses are at Rock Crest Glen in Mason City, Iowa including the Melson House [1913] the Schneider House [1914] the Rule House [1913] and the Page House [1913].

Marion Mahony, who was only the second woman to graduate in architecture from MIT, began working on and off for Frank Lloyd Wright in 1895. She met Griffin in this office and, when Wright moved to Europe in 1909, she took over the design completion role in his absence to discharge commissions in progress. In this capacity she arranged for Griffin to undertake some landscape design work. Their professional relationship progressed to a personal one and they married in 1911. Marion Mahony was a highly esteemed architectural drafter, whose perspective renderings enlivened both Griffin and Wright's designs in the Chicago period. They began their first big commission together in 1911 working on the Rock Crest Glen, Iowa project.

Soon after this they won the international design competition for Canberra and although the news reached them in May 1912, Griffin did not make his first trip to Australia until July of 1913. After his return to Chicago Griffin declined the position of head of Architecture at the University of Illinois at the end of 1913 and decided to move to Australia.

The Griffins based themselves in Melbourne close to the then Commonwealth administration. Although Walter held the position of Federal Capital Director of Design and Construction from 1914 to 1921, it was a part time appointment and he was only able to establish the road pattern of the city during that period. Fortunately quality projects including the Capital Theatre [1924] and Newman College [1918], remain in Melbourne. In 1924 the Griffins moved to Sydney and developed Castlecrag, overlooking Middle Harbour, where they built several houses as well as controlling the layout and development generally. With Eric Nicholls, in 1929, they became involved with the design and construction of municipal incinerators and a number of these are extant.

In 1935 the Griffins moved to India to the University of Lucknow and worked on several building designs before Walter died of peritonitis in 1937. Marion eventually returned to Chicago where she died 24 years later.

Canberra Architecture

Cuthbert Whitley (1886–1942)

When Cuthbert Whitley died in 1942 he was only 56, an age when many architects are still looking forward to years of productive activity. However in his short professional life, almost all of it working in the Commonwealth Public Service, Whitley became one of the key progenitors of Modernism, not only in Canberra but nationally.

His architectural training started in the State Public Works Department of Victoria as a drafter. In 1912, in his mid twenties, he moved to the Public Works Branch of the Commonwealth Department of Home Affairs in Melbourne as the most junior of six drafters. In 1920 he was promoted to the position of architect and worked closely with JS Murdoch, then Director-General of Works and Chief Architect, on the design and administration of the Commonwealth Bank project in Brisbane.

In August 1929 Whitley moved to Canberra with his family to work in the Department of Works and Railways under Principal Designing Architect Edwin Hubert Henderson. Using Henderson and Whitley's experience in bank design, the Works Branch collaborated with the Commonwealth Bank to execute bank projects throughout Australia. The architectural output of the Works Branch during the 1930s incorporated Classical and Art Deco mannerisms in the contemporary mode.

Cuthbert Whitley's Limestone Avenue house

By 1935, while Henderson took much of the Branch's administrative load, Whitley assumed responsibility for the architectural work. In 1936 during Henderson's absence overseas, Whitley designed the Ainslie Primary School, Canberra High School, the Patent Office and the Forrest Fire Station. The first manifestation of Whitley's full conversion to Modernism is the residences within this group that were radically re-designed in 1937. During 1939 Whitley designed the Modernist houses on Canberra and Limestone Avenues and also assumed the role of Acting Chief Architect for the second half of the year following Henderson's death in June.

War was declared in September 1939 and central staff of the Works Branch moved to Melbourne in November to become the executive wing of the Allied Works Council. The remaining Canberra staff worked on such projects as the completion of the Drill Hall at Acton, the Services Club at Manuka and RAAF buildings at Fairbairn. Whitley was involved in these projects as well as housing and other projects such as Barton House, and work for the completion of the Australian War Memorial.

John Smith Murdoch

Murdoch was the first Commonwealth Architect, although he never held that exact title and it is an office that no longer exists. His architectural stewardship saw Canberra through its first big construction boom in time for the opening of Parliament in May 1927. He is probably responsible for Walter Burley Griffin being in Australia at the beginning of the Great War when some had started to build Canberra without him and would probably have been happy not to have the American involved.

Murdoch appears to have been an officer of the Commonwealth almost from the time of its inception. From 1904 to 1914 he was Senior Assistant to the Director of Works, Department of Home Affairs, and obviously had an active interest in Canberra and was involved in the early infrastructure development of the new capital. Apart from designing some early works at Mt Stromlo, he prepared designs for the Kingston Power House in 1911 and then later, the Cotter Pumping Station [1915] and the Yarralumla Brickworks.

In December 1912, six months after the announcement of the competition results, Murdoch visited Walter Burley Griffin in Chicago alerting him to the Departmental Board's intention to start development of the city without him, and to a heavily modified plan. Griffin immediately protested and arranged a trip to Australia. It was Murdoch who greeted him on arrival in Sydney and accompanied him to the site.

From 1914 to 1919 Murdoch was Deputy Chief Architect in the Commonwealth Department of Works and Railways and Chief Architect from 1919 to 1929 as well as Director General of Works from 1927 to 1929. Like most senior Commonwealth bureaucrats he was Melbourne based at least until 1927, and in Murdoch's case until he retired in 1929. His Department was responsible for many Commonwealth Bank buildings in this period, notably in Brisbane. In Melbourne he was architect for the Commonwealth Offices [1912], the Mail Exchange [1913] and the High Court [1926]. In Canberra he is credited with Old Parliament House, the Hyatt Hotel Canberra, the Hotel Kurrajong and East and West Blocks, all finished at the time of Parliament moving up from Melbourne in 1927.

Malcolm Moir [1903–1971]

Malcom Moir spent practically his whole architectural career living and working in Canberra and is now recognised as one the city's pre-eminent Modernist architects.

He studied architecture under Leslie Wilkinson at the University of Sydney and graduated in 1924 at a time when the course was only turning out a handful of students each year. He worked first for the NSW Public Service and then in 1927 moved to Canberra to join the Architect's Department of the Federal Capital Commission. Working under HM Rolland, Moir is associated with the FCC's Alt Crescent group of houses in Ainslie – in fact he lived in one of them – and the Institute of Anatomy building in Acton [with Hayward Morris]. In early 1930 the Federal Government disbanded the FCC and handed the administration of the Territory back to the Department of Home Affairs.

Moir's own house in Melbourne Avenue, Forrest

Despite it being the Depression years, by 1931 Moir had established a private practice and was working as manager of Manuka's Capital Theatre. His greatest architectural accomplishment at this time was his own house in Melbourne Avenue [1934–36] which is central to the story of Modern Architecture in Canberra. By the late 1930s he was designing numerous houses for public servants, many of which survive. From 1938–39 he worked on the Evans Crescent group of houses with his second wife Heather Sutherland, also a former student of Wilkinsons at Sydney University.

Moir and Sutherland continued to work together until her death in 1953. After that the firm evolved into Moir Ward and Slater and then Moir and Slater in the 1960s.

Roy Grounds [1905–1981]

Roy Grounds was an eclectic, individualistic architect who emerged in an era when architects were trained outside the university system through indentureships. By the late 1920s he was in the United States on a travelling scholarship working in New York and Los Angeles, the latter at RKO Studios as a set designer. Upon his return to Melbourne he formed a partnership with Geoffrey Mewton that is now recognised as one of the early architectural practices to introduce Modernism to Australia. Key works of this period included Ground's own house at Mt Eliza, Victoria [1934] and, in the same year, the Stooke House at Brighton.

Between 1939 and 1942 Grounds, practising on his own, designed several significant apartment blocks. After the war he re-established his private practice and then from 1953 to 1962 was part of Grounds Romberg and Boyd. It was during this period that he produced the important Canberra works as well as another house for himself in Toorak [1954] and the tear-drop shaped James House in Kew [1955]. In 1959 Grounds won a commission to design the National Gallery of Victoria and Cultural Centre, and eventually left the partnership in 1962 to concentrate on this project which occupied him until his death in 1981.

Romaldo Giurgola [b 1920]

Romaldo Giurgola, son of an architect, former long time resident of the US and the architect of Parliament House is Canberra's best-known resident architect. He was born in Rome in 1920 and graduated from the University of Rome in 1949. He moved almost immediately to the United States and furthered his studies with a Masters of Architecture from Columbia University in 1951.

Giurgola's long career spans both academia and practice. In the years from 1954 to 1966 he was a Professor of Architecture at the University of Pennsylvania and from 1958 he worked in partnership with Ehrman Mitchell in Mitchell Giurgola Architects. Later he moved to New York after the firm expanded there in 1968. During this period he also taught at Columbia and was Chair of the School of Architecture from 1966 to 1971 and then Ware Professor of Architecture at Columbia since 1971. In Philadelphia, Giurgola had close contact with the architect/teacher Louis Kahn and published a monograph on this important architect's work in 1975. Kahn's modernistic rendering of the 19th century Beaux Arts architectural tradition interested Giurgola. Like Kahn he had been trained in that tradition and viewed architecture as more of an historic continuum emerging from the Italian Renaissance rather than a classical tradition that was breached by Modernism in the 20th century, as many do.

In his architectural work Giurgola regards process, the imperative to be free of fashion, the importance of 'place making' and what he calls the 'resonance of history', as significant in creating his particular sense of order.

Key buildings in his portfolio include the Wright Brothers Memorial Visitor's Centre [1960], the United Fund Building, Philadelphia [1971], Columbus East High School, Indiana [1972], Lang Music Building, Swarthmore [1973], MDRT Foundation Hall, Swarthmore College [1974], Tredyffrin Public Library, Pennsylvania [1976], The Life Sciences Building at Columbia [1977], Lafayette Place, Boston [1985] and Parliament House in Canberra [1988]. Giurgola moved permanently to Canberra in 1991 and took Australian citizenship in 1998.

Colin Madigan [b 1922]

For most of his career, which covers virtually the whole latter half of the 20th century, Colin ['Col'] Madigan was a principal of the Sydney firm Edwards Madigan Torzillo and Briggs. His early training at Sydney Technical College [then Sydney's only other architectural school, apart from Sydney University] was interrupted by World War II and not completed until 1950. While serving in the navy, Madigan's ship was aerially torpedoed and he was one of only a handful to survive a traumatic sinking and lengthy exposure before rescue.

In 1954 Madigan became a partner in the practice and initially flirted with cool, Miesian forms such as his own house in Narrabeen. However his work gradually evolved to the sculptural and monumental, using heavy, fortress-like forms that were cut away, sliced and manipulated to admit natural light. Beginning with the Warringah Library [Sulman Award, 1966], the Bathurst Students' Residence [Sulman Award, 1970] and then the High Court and the National Gallery in Canberra, we find a sequence of work that constitutes a corpus of monumental public architecture equal to any in the country during the same period.

Col Madigan was awarded the RAIA Gold Medal in 1981.

Harry Seidler [b 1923]

Harry Seidler's architecture exhibits a disciplined use of geometry, rational building planning, a forthright expression of structure and construction, and a sensibility to elements of 20th century, and even Baroque, art – this latter a more recent occurrence.

Seidler was born in Vienna in 1923, but left with his family in 1938 following the German annexation of Austria. With the onset of war he was interned in England and eventually sent to the Canadian prairies in 1941. He completed architectural studies at the University of Manitoba in 1944 where he received a scholarship to undertake Gropius' postgraduate architecture program at Harvard. Thereafter he came into contact with Josef Albers at Black Mountain College in 1946 and worked in Marcel Breuer's New York office from 1946–48. Before coming to Australia, Seidler also spent time working with Oscar Niemeyer in Rio de Janeiro.

In 1949 Harry Seidler arrived in Sydney and gained a reputation for innovation and uncompromising modernity in the face of some initial resistance to his work. His corpus of work is vast, including the Rose Seidler House, Turramurra [1950], Australia Square, Sydney [1961], his own house, Killara [1967], MLC Centre, Sydney [1972], Grosvenor Place, Sydney [1982], Shell HQ, Melbourne [1985], the Horizon Apartments, Darlinghurst [1990] and, at the end of the century, a large public housing development in Vienna.

Enrico Taglietti [b 1926]

Italian born Taglietti has dedicated most of his architectural life to Canberra and, through his corpus of work is one of the city's most important post-war figures. Detached from his native Milan at the age of 12, he spent his high school years in Eritrea. At age 20 he was studying architecture back in Milan where his teachers included such luminaries as Gio Ponti, Franco Albini, Marco Zanuso, Bruno Zevi and Pier Luigi Nervi. Of these, Zevi's critical vision of Wrightian organic architectural spatial poetics, appears to have been the most relevant in nurturing Taglietti's architectural development. In particular its blend of modernist spatiality and aesthetics.

In 1954, one year after graduating and while attending a Summer School with Le Corbusier in Marseilles, Taglietti began working as co-ordinator of foreign entries to the Milan Triennale. There he made contact with figures such as Aalto, Niemeyer and Buckminster Fuller. The following year Taglietti brought an exhibition of Italian Architecture, Design and Fashion to Australia for the David Jones department store and visited Canberra with a brief to find a site for a new Italian Embassy. He reacted to the small (15,000) population of the capital at that time with a mixture of shock and optimism: '… the city untouched by ugliness or history. The voids, the boundless spaces, the vision of the invisible city, the inhuman overwhelming silence, the infinity and eternity revealed.'

Taglietti found the site, built the Embassy in the early 1960s and, apart from brief interludes in Melbourne and back in Milan, has been in Canberra ever since. He saw Canberra as being an 'invisible city' waiting to be made manifest by works of architecture. This vision has sustained him, muse-like, ever since as he produced a series of distinctive residential designs in the city's green-field suburbs, as well as office buildings, churches and institutional buildings in its more central areas. Taglietti has published his work and lectured in many parts of the world including Europe, Asia and North America as well as Australia.

John Andrews [b 1933]

John Andrews's professional activities have yielded significant works of architecture in the USA, Canada and Australia.

Born and raised at Gordon on Sydney's North Shore, Andrews graduated from Sydney University in 1956 and immediately undertook postgraduate studies at Harvard under the Spanish Modernist Jose Luis Sert.

In 1958 his entry in the Toronto City Hall competition received a second place and he moved to Canada to work, initially for the Finnish architect Viljo Revell [who won the competition]. Andrews stayed in Toronto for the next 17 years, establishing a successful practice, teaching at the University of Toronto [he eventually chaired the Department of Architecture] and expanded his client base into the USA. Key works of his North American phase include Scarborough College [1964], the Seaport Passenger Terminal in Miami [1967], Gund Hall, Harvard University [1968] and the CN Tower in Toronto [1977].

Callam Offices [former Woden TAFE College] Easty Street, Phillip, by John Andrews

Andrews returned to Australia at the invitation of the National Capital Development Commission in the late 1960s and accepted their offer to design Cameron Offices, Belconnen [1976], and later he designed the student residences at UC and ANU. Other notable works in Australia include the American Express Tower, Sydney [1976] and the Chemistry Building at the University of Queensland [1975].

In all these works Andrews displayed a concern for design process characterised by rational analysis, the production of simple, geometric plan and section types, and robust concrete and masonry construction. He was uninterested in fashion, rather he was concerned to find the 'right' outcome working from first principles in each commission.

Tours

Canberra Architecture

Tours

Although Canberra seems spread out, few suburbs can be said to be really distant because of the excellent roads and bus transport system. However having located the suburb you wish to visit, the frequent curving crescents and circuits often tend to disorientate visitors. To overcome this we recommend you select one constant marker near the area you are visiting, such as the flagpole on Parliament House, the Telstra tower on Black Mountain, or Lake Burley Griffin, and in this way you should be able to define your location.

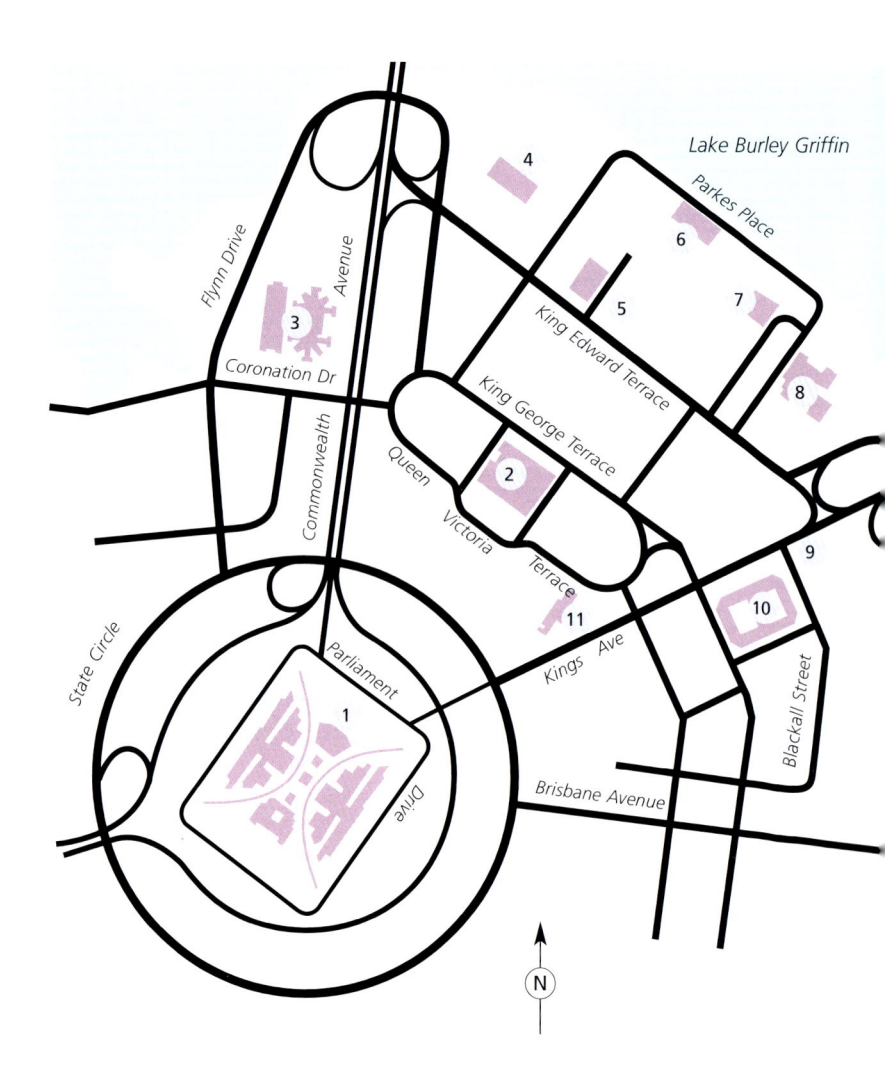

Central National Area

It is advisable to start this tour at Parliament House. Apart from the building itself, which merits a visit of at least one hour, there are regular guided tours, and it is possible to walk right over the top of the Parliament building, thus putting the politicians firmly in their place. In this process the visitor will gain a panoramic view of the area prior to moving on to view other buildings on this tour. From Parliament House it is all downhill, first to Old Parliament House, then west to the Hyatt Hotel before heading towards Lake Burley Griffin and the major public buildings spread along the lakeshore. Light refreshments and toilet facilities are available at Questacon, the High Court and the National Gallery.

1. *Parliament House* [1]
   Parliament Drive
   Mitchell Giurgola Thorp

2. *Old Parliament House* [2]
   King George Terrace
   JS Murdoch

3. *Hyatt Hotel,* [9]
   Commonwealth Avenue
   JS Murdoch and Daryl Jackson

4. *National Library of Australia* [7]
   King Edward Terrace
   Bunning and Madden with TE O'Mahoney

5. *Questacon* [6]
   King Edward Terrace
   Lawrence Nield

6. *Commonwealth Place and Reconciliation Place* [8]
   Parkes Place
   Durback Bloch, Sue Barnsley, Simon Kringas

7. *High Court of Australia* [5]
   King Edward Terrace
   Col Madigan, Chris Kringas [EMT&B]

8. *National Gallery of Australia* [4]
   Parkes Place
   Col Madigan [EMT&B], Andrew Andersons [addition]

9. *Australian Centre for Christianity & Culture* [14]
   Kings Avenue
   James Grose [Bligh Voller Nield]

10. *Edmund Barton Offices* [11]
    Kings Avenue
    Harry Seidler,

11. *National Archives, East Block* [3]
    Queen Victoria Terrace
    JS Murdoch

Parliament House

Hyatt Hotel

National Library

High Court

National Gallery

Edmund Barton Offices

Canberra Architecture

Canberra City [Civic] West Canberra

This tour is usually made on foot because the distances are not great and you will thereby avoid the problem of city parking. There is a bus route through the University campus which can be used to return to the city at the end of the tour.

Start the tour at City Square and proceed along London Circuit in a northwesterly direction, crossing Northbourne Avenue at the colonnaded Sydney and Melbourne Buildings and then keep heading towards the west.

Sydney + Melbourne Buildings

Canberra School of Art

Canberra School of Music

Shine Dome Becker Hall

ScreenSound Australia

1. *Civic Offices and Square* [17]
   London Circuit at Civic Square
   Roy Simpson [Yunken Freeman], MGT, May Flannery and Hassel

2. *Sydney + Melbourne Buildings* [18]
   London Circuit at Northbourne Avenue
   Sulman, Kirkpatrick and Limburg

3. *ACT Magistrates Court* [26]
   Knowles Place
   MCC Architects

4. *Law Courts of the ACT* [24]
   Knowles Place
   Roy Simpson, Yunken Freeman

5. *ACT Police Headquarters* [25]
   16–18 London Circuit
   Hassel McConnel

6. *ANZ Bank* [23]
   17 London Circuit
   Stuart McIntosh

7. *Reserve Bank of Australia* [22]
   20–22 London Circuit
   Howlett and Bailey

8. *Canberra School of Music* [21]
   Childers Street, Acton
   Daryl Jackson and Evan Walker

9. *Canberra School of Art* [20]
   Ellery Crescent and Childers Street, Acton
   Cuthbert Whitley/Daryl Jackson

10. *Shine Dome Becker Hall* [19]
    Gordon Street and McCoy Circuit, Acton
    Grounds, Romberg and Boyd

11. *ScreenSound Australia* [27]
    McCoy Circuit and Liversidge Street, Acton
    Walter Hayward Morris and GHD Architects

12. *ANU University House* [28]
    Balmain Crescent and Liversidge Street, Acton
    Brian Lewis

Tours: Canberra City [Civic] West Canberra

ACT Magistrates Court

163

Acknowledgements

Our thanks go to the following individuals and organisations for the provision of materials, accommodation, information and editorial assistance:

David Headon, Vickie Hingston-Jones, Les Flynn
National Capital Authority

Ann Barr, Loreana Sipos
Canberra Tourism and Events Corporation

Major Robert Morrison
Royal Military College of Australia

Claire Tedeschi
Government House

National Archives of Australia
National Library of Australia

Enrico Taglietti, Col Madigan, Romaldo Giurgola, Harry Seidler, Philip Goad, John Nutt, Sally Milner, Dr Jim Carson, Alastair Swayn, John Blue, Gavin Blue, Ben Hall, Michael Smart, Vince Ford, Geoffrey Quayle, Veronica Owens

Galvanised iron cow by Jeff Thompson on lawn of NZ High Commission

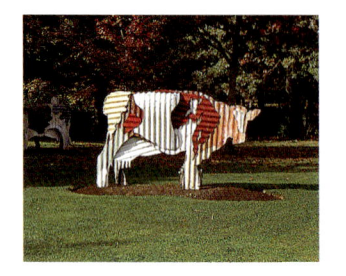

Index

A

ANU [Australian National University] 61, 62, 63
Australian Centre for Christianity and Culture 41, *41* 106
Australian Construction Services 119
Australian Defence Force Academy [ADFA] 73
Australian Federal Police Building 56, *56*
Australian Forestry School 96
Australian Geological Survey Organisation HQ [AGSO] 119, *119*
Australian Institute of Sport 129, 131, *132*
Australian Institute of Urban Studies 35
Australian National Archives 11, *32*, *32*
Australian National Botanic Gardens 69
Australian National Gallery 155, see also National Gallery of Australia
Australian National University [ANU] 61, 62, 63
Australian National University 78, 101, 134, 135, 147, 158
Australian War Memorial 14, 21, 29, 42, *42*, 43 79, 81, 140, 150

B

Bacon, Edmund 12
Baillie-Scott, MH 96, 111
Banks, Joseph 69
Baptist Church and Manse 106, *106*
Barnett Close, 122
Barnett, Paul 117
Barnsley, Sue 37
Barr, John 39
Barry, Charles 30

Barwick, Garfield 34
Bass, Tom 63
Bathurst Students' Residence 155
Baur, Hans Peter 93
Baur, Hermann 93
Bean, CE 42
Beauchamp Street 97
Behrens, Peter 108
Belconnen Library 136, *136*
Benjamin House 98, *98*
Benwell, Stephen 29
Berg, Pamille 141
Berlin Building Exhibition 86
Bimbimbie, VC's residence 133, *133*
Birrell, James 98
Bishop, Tony 27, 29
Black Mountain 11, 67, 69, 77, 97, 129
Black Mountain College 156
Black Mountain Nature Reserve 61
Blacket, Edmund 80
Blamey Crescent 78
Blau, Robin 28
Bligh Voller Nield 36, 41
Bloch, Durbach 37. See Durbach, Bloch
Blount house 148, *148*
Blue house 123, *123*
Blue, Shane 123
Blundells Cottage 74
Bolt, Dirk 91, 97,118
Botanic Gardens, Sydney 67
Bourne, Rachel 123
Bowden House 98, *98*
Bowden, Bruce 76
Bowe and Burroughs 118
Boyd, Arthur 27, 29
Boyd, Robin 52, 77, 91, 92, 101, 103, 118
Brack, John 29

Breuer, Marcel 156
Bridges, William Throsby 69
Brindabella Ranges 81, 118, 125
Bruce Stadium 131, *131*
Bruce O'Connor Ridge 129
Brunelleschi, Filippo 51
Bunning and Madden 36
Bunning, Walter 36
Burcham Clamp and Finch 38, 104
Burgess, Greg 117
Burgmann, Bishop 108
Burnham, Daniel 13
Butt, Ric 147
Butters, John 106

C

Cachemaille-Day, Welch 108
Callam Offices 121
Calthorpes' House 110, *110*
Cameron Chisholm and Nicol 41, 122
Cameron Offices 136, 137, *137*, 138 158
Camp Hill 30, 33
Campbell family 73, 74
Campbell group 95
Campbell, Frederick 40
Campbell, George 74, 80
Campbell, Marianne 74
Campbell, Robert 74, 80
Canberra Avenue 110
Canberra Centre 49
Canberra Grammar School 104, *104*
Canberra High School 53, 84, 150
Canberra Hospital Diagnostic and Treatment Building 120, *120*
Canberra Museum and Gallery [CMAG] 50

165

Canberra Nature Park 73, 79, 123
Canberra Post Office 32
Canberra School of Art [Canberra High School] 53, *53*
Canberra School of Music 54, *54*
Canberra Stadium 131, *131*, 132
Canberra Theatre 50
Canberra Valley 13
Canberry 62
Capital Hill 15, 21, 25, 33, 91
Capital Jet Facility 76, *76*
Capital Theatre 149, 152
Capitol, The 11
Carillon. See National Carillon
Caroline Chisholm High School 124, *124*
Carter house 148
Casboulte, R 116
Cater House 106, *106*
Cathedral Hill 107
Cazneaux, Harold 29
Centenary of Federation, Council of 52
Central National Area 21
Chancery building 40, *40*
Changi Chapel 69, *75*
Chemistry Building, University of Queensland 158
Chifley, Ben 30
Citadel 11
City design competition 9, 10, 13
City Hall 11
City Hill 49, 50, 56
Civic Centre 51
Civic Offices and Square 50, *50*
Civic Theatre 99
Civic Zone Substation 68, *68*

Clamp and Son, Burcham 108
Clark House, Dymphna and Manning 101
Clark, Dymphna 101
Clark, Manning 101, 103, 118
Clough, Richard 40
Clynes House 95, *95*
CN Tower, Toronto 158
Cobby Street 79
Collard Clarke and Jackson 64, 65
Columbia University 25, 154
Columbus East High School, Indiana 154
Colvin Street 118
Commonwealth Architects office 119
Commonwealth Bank 150
Commonwealth Department of Works 30
Commonwealth Offices 151
Commonwealth Park 21
Commonwealth Public Service 150
Condell Street 138
Constitution, The 7
Cook, James 69
Cooley House 148
Cooper, Anthony 94
Corbusier, Le 44, 157
Cotter Pumping Station 151
Council of the Academy 52
Cox Humphries Moss 95
Cox, Philip 81, 91, 93, 122, 129, 131, 132, 147
Crozier Circuit 123
Crust, John 42, 43
CSIRO 61, 96, 110
Discovery Centre 67, *67*, 135

FC Pye Laboratories 68, *68*
Phytotron Building 69, *69*
Cultural Centre 153
Cunningham, Andrew and Jane 125
Cuppacumbalong 124, 125, *125*

D

D'Lisle, Viscount 80
David Jones department store 157
de Salis 125
De Stijl group 111
Denton Corker Marshall 42, 43, 147
Department of Architecture 158
Department of Home Affairs 151, 152
Department of Housing and Construction 76
Department of Interior Works 50, 53, 84, 102, 110, 147
Department of Works 116
Department of Works and Railways 84, 150, 151
Desbrowe-Annear, Harold 91, 96
Dickson Library 87, *87*
Dingle [DeQuetteville] House 117, *117*
Dirrawan Gardens 80
Dodgshun Court 138, *138*
Doesburg, Theo van 111
Doonkuna Street 81
Dowse, Sara 32
Drake Brockman Drive 139
Drill Hall 150
Dryandra Street 78, 212
Dudok, Willem 108
Duffield, WG 116
Dumbrell, Leslie 29
Dunn, Richard 29
Dunrossil, Viscount 80

Index

Duntroon [Royal Military College] 40, 67, 69, 73, 74, 75, 80
Duntroon Dairy 74
Duntroon House 74, *74*
Dupain, Max 29
Durbach, Bloch 37
Dysart, Michael 123

E

East and West Blocks 21, *21,* 151
East-West Municipal Axis 51
Edinburgh, Duke of 63
Edmondson Street 78
Edmond & Corrigan 147
Edmund Barton Offices 39, *39*
Edwards Madigan Torzillo and Briggs 33, 34, 155
Eggcrate residences 66, 134, *134*
Eggleston MacDonald 119
Elimatta Street 81
Embassy of
 Finland 93, 94, *94*
 Ireland 93, *93*
 Italy 87, 157
 Japan 92
 Mexico 93, 94, *94*
 Russia 109
 Sweden [Royal Swedish Legation] 63, 92, *92*
 Switzerland 93, *93*
Emery house 148
Emu Ridge 138
English Scottish and Australian Bank 55, *55*
Evans Crescent 109, 152

F

Fallingwater house 55
Federal Capital Advisory Committee [FCAC] 51, 99, 106, 111
Federal Capital Commission, 39, 62, 80, 82, 147, 152
Federal Capital 7
Federal Golf Course 117, 121
Fenner House 103, *103*
Fenner, Frank 103, 118
Ferguson, Anne 27
Fitzgerald Street 95
Fire Station, ACT 102, *102*
Flannery, May 50
Forrest Conservation Area 99
Forrest Fire Station 102, *102,* 150
Fowell Mansfield and MacLurcan 75
Frankel, Otto 79
French, Leonard 36
Fuller Street 97
Fuller, Buckminster 157
Furneaux Street 111

G

Gallipoli 69
Gascoigne, Rosalie 116
Gawler Crescent 98
Gazetted Plan 53
Gazzard, Marea 28
Geerilong Gardens 80
GHD Architects 62
Gibson, Robin 129, 136, 147
Gilroy, Cardinal 107
Giralang Primary School 139, *139*
Giurgola, Romaldo 25, 82, 129, 133, 134, 141, 147, 154
Glancy and son, Clement 107
Gorton, John, building 21, 36
Government House [Yarralumla] 40, *40*

Graduate Management Programs Facility, ANU 64, *64*
Graduate Program in Public Policy 64
Graduate School of Design, Harvard 137
Grahame, Kenneth 66
Grandstand and Amenities Building, ADFA 76, *76*
Griffin, Marion Mahony, competition 116
Griffin plan, the 11, 12, 15, 21, 56
Griffin, Marion Mahony 99, 147, 148, 149
Griffin, R 148
Griffin, Walter Burley 9–11, 25, 30 49-51, 53, 61, 67, 69, 82, 91, 99, 108, 147, 148, 149,151
Gropius, Walter 156
Grose, James 41
Grosvenor Place, Sydney 156
Grounds Romberg and Boyd 52, 68, 69, 77, 79, 85, 92, 100, 101, 147, 153
Grounds, Roy 52, 68, 73, 77, 79, 91, 92, 100, 101, 153
Gudgenby River 125
Guelph University 66
Guida, Hal 82
Gund Hall 137
Gund Hall, Harvard University 158
Gungahlin 129
Gunn, Graeme 138

H

Harrison, Peter 12
Harry, Pat 50
Harvard University 156, 158
Haskell, John 39
Hassel Architects 50

167

Hassel McConnel 56
Hawke, Bob 63
Heikkinen and Komonen 94
Henderson, Edwin Hubert 53, 83, 84, 102, 150
High Court 21, *21,* 33, 34, 36, 37, 151, 155
Hilversum School 108
Hirvonen-Huttenen 94
Hoechst Buildings 108
Hogan, Paul 122
Holford, Sir William 14, 15
Holy Trinity Lutheran National Memorial Church 85, *85*
Hopetoun Circuit, 95
Horizon Apartments, Darlinghurst 95,156
Hotel Kurrajong 151
Howard, Ebenezer 10
Howard, Harry 33, 34
Howard, John 35
Humphries, Graeme 57, 147
Hyatt Hotel 38, *38,* 151
Hyde Park Barracks, Sydney 67
Hyson Green Clinic 131, *131*

I

Information Sciences and Engineering Building 134
Institute of Anatomy 14, *14,* 152

J

Jack, Russell 106
Jackson, Daryl 38, 53, 54, 64, 67, 76 129, 132, 133, 135, 138, 147
Jaeger Building, ANU 64
James house 153
James, John 125

Jeffreys, Lieutenant Arthur 62
Jelinek 91, 98
Jerildrie Court 81
Johnson, Roger 34
Joint House Department 25

K

Kahn, Louis 154
Kerr, John 40
Killara house 156
King George Tower 121 see also American Express Tower
Kings Park 21
Kingston Power House 151
Kirkpatrick and Limburg 51
Klenze, Leo von 31
Klippel, Robert 29
Kringas, Chris 34
Kringas, Simon 37

L

Lafayette Place, Boston 154
Lake Burley Griffin 21, 67, 73, 77, 81, 91, 122
Lake Ginninderra 129, 135
Lake Ginninderra College 135, *135*
Lander's St Saviour 108
Lane-Pool, Charles 96
Lang Music Building, Swarthmore 154
Langley, Warren 28
Lanyon Homestead 125, *125*
Law Courts of the ACT 49, 56, *56*
Laurence, Janet 43
Le Corbusier 54, 100
Legislative Assembly, ACT 15, 50
Leichhardt Street, 110
Lewis, Brian 63
Life Sciences Building, Columbia 154

Limburg, D 111
Limestone Avenue 107, 84
Limestone Cottage 74, *74*
Llewellyn Hall 54
Lodge, the 110
Longfellow, Henry Wadsworth 8
Lundquist, EGH 63, 92
Lutyens, Edwin 31
Lynn, Elwyn 29
Lyons, Joe 107

M

Madigan, Colin 33, 34, 147, 155
Magistrates Court, ACT 57, *57*
Mahony, Marion 10, 12, 82
Maiden, Joseph 67
Mail Exchange 151
Majura homestead 74
Marriot House 101
Martin, Mandy 28
Massachusetts Institute of Technology 148
MCC Architects 57
McIntosh, Stuart 55
McKay, Ian 93, 122
MDRT Foundation Hall, Swarthmore College 154
Meier, Richard 118
Melbourne Avenue 99
Melbourne Exhibition Building 28
Melson House 148
Menzies, Robert Gordon ['Bob'] 36, 107
Mewton, Geoffrey 52, 153
MGM Studios 52
MGT 133
Milan Triennale 157
MIT, Massachusetts 52

Index

Mitchell Giurgola and Thorp 25, 27, 28, 42, 50, 54, 82, 94, 141, 154
Mitchell, Ehrman 154
MLC Centre, Sydney 156
Mockridge Circuit 139
Moir and Slater 152
Moir House 99, *99*
Moir, Angus 99
Moir, Malcolm 78, 91, 99, 109, 147, 152
Molonglo River 11, 13
MoMA 'International Style' exhibition 84
Monaro Crescent 103
Mondrian, Piet 110, 111
Moorcroft, Rommel 94
Morphett Street 86
Morris, Walter Hayward 62, 152
Morris, William 96
Mortlock, Bryce 102
Moss, Rodney 57, 95, 131, 147
Mount Ainslie 11, 21, 43, 50, 77, 79, 81
Mount Pleasant 21, 69
Mount Stromlo 151
Mount Stromlo Observatory 115, 116, *116*
Mugga Mugga homestead 74
Mugga Way 106, 110
Munns Sly Scott-Bohana Moss 131
Murcutt, Glenn 119
Murdoch, John Smith 30, 32, 38, 42, 83, 84, 116, 147, 150, 151, *151*
Murrumbidgee River 115, 124, 125

N

National Association [RAIA HQ] 102, *102*
National Athletic Stadium 131, *131*
National Botanical Gardens 61
National Bushfire Research Unit 96
National Capital Authority 15, 37, 73
National Capital Development Commission [NCDC] 15, 36, 49, 56, 100, 122, 137, 138, 147, 158
National Carillon 41, *41*, 122
National Estate 67
National Film and Sound Archive 62, *62*
National Gallery of Australia 21, *21*, 33, 34, 36
National Gallery of Victoria 153
National Library of Australia 21, *21*, 33, 34, 36, 37
National Museum of Australia 21, 29, *29*, 44, 45
National Prisoner-of-War memorial 69, *69*
National Science and Technology Centre 35, 36
National Seventh Day Adventist Church 85, *85*
National Sports Swimming Centre 132, 133, *133*, 135
National Triangle 21
Nervi, Pier Luigi 157
Nervi's Olympic Hall 52
New Directions In Japanese Architecture 92

Newman College 149
Ngunnawal language 125
Ngunnawal people 62
Nicholls, Eric 149
Nield, Laurence 35, 120, 124, 147
Niemeyer, Oscar 156
Nolan, Sidney 29
North Building 50
Northbourne Avenue 86
Northcote Street 98
Norwood Park Crematorium 140, *140*
NSW Public Service 152

O

O'Mahoney, TE 36
O'Malley, King 7, 8, 9, 12
Oak Park studio 148
Oakley and Parkes 99, 110
Old Parliament House, 30, *30*, 31, 32, 151
Old Parliament House Gardens, 21
Oldroyd, Graham 27
Oliphant, Kenneth 110
Olsen, John 29
Orana School for Rudolf Steiner Education 117, *117*
Oud, JJP 111

P

Page House 148
Page, Phil 147
Parliament Act [1974] 25
Parliament House 11, *11*, 13, *13*, 15, 21, 25-29, 32, 35, 77, 81, 83, 141, 154
Parliament House Gardens 21
Parliament, Federal 7-9
Parliamentary Library 30, 36
Parliamentary Zone 21, 34, 35, 36, 37, 91

169

Patent Office 150
Paterson House 130, *130*
Pauline Griffin Building, ANU 65, *65*
Peddle, Thorp & Walker 92
Pegrum, Anthony 130
Pegrum, Roger 40, 51, 130, 147
Pena,Terrazas de la 94
Peplow, FW 106
Peregian Roadhouse, Noosa 98
Perkins, Kevin 28
Peter Karmel Building 54
Petit and Sevitt 121
Petit House 121
Petit, Brian 121
Phillips, Cheryl 28
Pialligo 73. 74
Pilbara Place 122, *122*
Playhouse Theatre 50
Police Building, ACT 56, *56*
Ponti, Gio 157
Pool of Reflection 43, *43*
Prairie School 10, 31, 38, 148
Presbyterian Church of St Andrew 39, *39*
Pryor, Anthony 29
Pryor, Lindsay 103
Public Works 150

Q
Queen Elizabeth 25, 35, 40, 41
Questacon 35, *35*, 37

R
RAAF buildings 150
RAIA Gold Medal 155
RAIA Headquarters 102, *102*
Raiders football team 50
Ramsden, Michael 27
raumplan 130
Reconciliation Place 37, *37*

Red Hill 21
Reid Urban Conservation Area 80
Reid, John 124
Research School of Earth Sciences 64
Reserve Bank Building 56
Reserve Bank of Australia 49
Retter, Michael 27, 29
Revell, Viljo 158
RG Menzies Building, ANU 65, *65*
Richardson 'Bridge' house 101
Ricker, Nathan 148
Rietveld, Gerrit 110, 111
Rijsdijk, Mezza 28
RKO Studios 52, 153
Robert Peck von Hartel Trethowan 44
Roberts, Tom 28
Rock Crest Glen 149
Rohe, Mies van der 110
Rolland, HM 82, 116, 152
Roman Catholic Cathedral 107
Romberg, Frederic 52
Rome Olympics 52
Rose Seidler House, Turramurra 63, 156
Roseman, Hastings and Soret 140
Rosenthal, Charles 42
Rowe Place 122
Royal Canberra Hospital 45
Rudd, L 111
Rude Timber Buildings in Australia 93
Rudolph, Paul 54
Rule House 148
Ryrie Street, No.2 79, *79*

S
Saarinen's Kresge Auditorium 52

Sakamaki, T 92
Scarborough College 137, 158
Scarborough, J 65
Schinkel, KF 31
Schneider House 148
School of Architecture 154
School of Art 84
Science Centre 21
ScreenSound Australia 62, *62*, 64
Scullin, James 107
Seaport Passenger Terminal, Miami 158
Seidler, Harry 39, 63, 78, 79, 91, 95, 98, 147, 156
Senate porte cochère 27, *27*
Senate Select Committee 50
Sert, Jose Luis 158
Services Club 150
Seventh Day Adventist Church, see National Seventh Day Adventist Church, 85
Shell HQ, Melbourne 156
Shine Dome Becker Hall, Australian Academy of Science 52, *52*, 64
Shine, Professor John 52
Simpson, Roy 50, 56, 104, 147
Sir Roland Wilson Building 64, *64*
Sloane house 148
Snow, Terry 76
Snowy Mountains Scheme 98
Soares, Alberto Dias 74, 80
Sodersten, Emil 42, 43
Soret, Peter 140
South Building 50
Spelman, Philip 50
St Christopher's RC Cathedral 107, *107*

Index

St John's Church 74, 80, *80*, 108
St Paul's Church of England 108, *108*
St Thomas Aquinas Church 141, *141*
Stapley Courts 138
State Public Works Department 150
Steiner, Rudolf 117
Steinway Hal 148
Stephenson and Turner 120
Stewart, Colin 57, 147
Stinson Library 148
Stones, Ellis 138
Stooke House 153
Sullivan, Louis 148
Sullivan's creek 66
Sulman Award 63, 155
Sulman, John 51, 67, 99
Sulman, Kirkpatrick and Limburg 51
Supreme Court, ACT 56, *56*
Sutherland, Heather 109, 152
Swayn, Alastair 64, 67, 76, 132, 147
Swinger Hill 122, *122*
Sydney and Melbourne Buildings 51, *51*
Sydney School 102, 106, 122
Sydney Technical College 155

T

Taglietti, Enrico 87, 91, 105, 117, 129, 130, 139, 140, 141, 147, 157
Tai, Keak 116
Tange, Kenzo 92
Tasmania Circle 100
Taylor, Jennifer 36
Taylor, Peter 28

Telstra tower 77
Tharwa Bridge 125
Therapeutic Goods Administration Building TGA 119, *119*
Thomson, Ann 29
Tjakamarra, Michael Nelson 27, 29
Toad Hall, ANU 66, *66*, 121, 134
Tocal College 122
Tomb of the Unknown Soldier 43
Tonkin Zulaikha Harford 42
Toronto City Hall competition 158
Torrens Street, No. 65 84
Tran, Hai 116
Tredyffrin Public Library, Pennsylvania 154
Trickett Street 139
Tucker, Albert 29

U

Union, ANU 65
United Fund Building, Philadelphia 154
University, Australian National [ANU] 61, 62, 63
University House, ANU 63, *63*
University Library 65
University of California 52
University of Canberra 129, 133, 134, 158
University of Illinois 148, 149
University of Lucknow 149
University of Manitoba 156
University of Melbourne 63
University of Pennsylvania 154
University of Queensland 158
University of Rome 154
University of Sydney 152, 155, 158

University of Toronto 158
Urambi Village Co-operative 123, *123*
Usonian houses 55
Utzon, Jorn 130

V

Vasey Crescent, houses 42, 44, 46 77, *77*
Venturi, Robert 133
Victoria, Queen 8
Victorian Arts Centre commission 77
Victorian Modern: 111 Years of Modern Architecture in the State of Victoria, Australia 101
Vojsk, Milan 49
Voysey, CFA 96
Vreeland, Thomas 133

W

Wakefield Avenue 86
Walker, Evan 54
Waller Crescent 11, 78
Walling, Edna 40
Ward, Fred 63
Ward, Neville 78
Warringah Library 155
Waterhouse family 110
Waterhouse, Doug 110
West Block 32
Weston Creek 67
Weston, Charles 67
Westridge House 96, 111
Whitlam, Gough 40, 104
Whitley, Cuthbert 53, 83, 84, 91, 102, 110, 111, 147, 150
Wilkinson, Leslie 42, 152
Williams, Fred 29
Wilson House 130, *130*
Winston, Denis 86
Woden Valley Hospital 120, *120*

171

Wolseley, John 29
Woods Bagot 136
Woolley, Ken 68, 85, 91, 102, 121, 147
Wright Brothers Memorial Visitor's Centre 154
Wright, David 28
Wright, Frank Lloyd 10, 38, 55, 148, 149
Wright, John and Mary 125
Wright, William 125

Y

Yarralumla Brickworks 151
Yarralumla Homestead 40
York, Duke of 30
Yuncken Freeman 50, 56, 104

Z

Zanuso, Marco 157
Zevi, Bruno 157
Zimmer, Klaus 28

Pear [version No. 2] by George Baldessin, cor-ten steel, National Gallery of Australia